PEEPS AT MANY LANDS

ANCIENT EGYPT, "A LAND OF OLD RENOWN"

BY REV. JAMES BAIKIE, F.R.A.S.

AUTHOR OF "PEEPS AT THE HEAVENS" AND "THE STORY OF THE PHARAOHS"

Originally published in 1912.

CONTENTS

ANCIENT EGYPT

CHAPTER I

"A LAND OF OLD RENOWN"

If we were asked to name the most interesting country in the world, I suppose that most people would say Palestine--not because there is anything so very wonderful in the land itself, but because of all the great things that have happened there, and above all because of its having been the home of our Lord. But after Palestine, I think that Egypt would come next. For one thing, it is linked very closely to Palestine by all those beautiful stories of the Old Testament, which tell us of Joseph, the slave-boy who became Viceroy of Egypt; of Moses, the Hebrew child who became a Prince of Pharaoh's household; and of the wonderful exodus of the Children of Israel.

But besides that, it is a land which has a most strange and wonderful story of its own. No other country has so long a history of great Kings, and wise men, and brave soldiers; and in no other country can you see anything to compare with the great buildings, some of them most beautiful, all of them most wonderful, of which Egypt has so many. We have some old and interesting buildings in this country, and people go far to see cathedrals and castles that are perhaps five or six hundred years old, or even more; but in Egypt, buildings of that age are looked upon as almost new, and nobody pays very much attention to them. For the great temples and tombs of Egypt were, many of them, hundreds of years old before the story of our Bible, properly speaking, begins.

The Pyramids, for instance, those huge piles that are still the wonder of the world, were far older than any building now standing in Europe, before Joseph was sold to be a slave in Potiphar's house. Hundreds upon hundreds of years before anyone had ever heard of the Greeks and the Romans, there were great Kings reigning in Egypt, sending out their armies to conquer Syria and the Soudan, and their ships to explore the unknown southern seas, and wise men were writing books which we can still read. When Britain was a wild, unknown island, inhabited only by savages as fierce and untaught as the South Sea Islanders, Egypt was a great and highly civilized country, full of great cities, with noble palaces and temples, and its people were wise and learned.

So in this little book I want to tell you something about this wonderful and interesting old country, and about the kind of life that people lived in it in those days of long ago, before most other lands had begun to waken up, or to have any history at all. First of all, let us try to get an idea of the land itself. It is a very remarkable thing that so many of the countries which have played a great part in the history of the world have been small countries. Our own Britain is not very big, though it has had a great story. Palestine, which has done more than any other country to make the world what it is to-day, was called "the least of all lands." Greece, whose influence comes, perhaps, next after that of Palestine, is only a little hilly corner of Southern

Europe. And Egypt, too, is comparatively a small land.

It looks a fair size when you see it on the map; but you have to remember that nearly all the land which is called Egypt on the map is barren sandy desert, or wild rocky hill-country, where no one can live. The real Egypt is just a narrow strip of land on either side of the great River Nile, sometimes only a mile or two broad altogether, never more than thirty miles broad, except near the mouth of the river, where it widens out into the fan-shaped plain called the Delta. Someone has compared Egypt to a lily with a crooked stem, and the comparison is very true. The long winding valley of the Nile is the crooked stem of the lily, and the Delta at the Nile mouth, with its wide stretch of fertile soil, is the flower; while, just below the flower, there is a little bud--a fertile valley called the Fayum.

Long before even Egyptian history begins, there was no bloom on the lily. The Nile, a far bigger river then than it is now, ran into the sea near Cairo, the modern capital of Egypt; and the land was nothing but the narrow valley of the river, bordered on either side by desert hills. But gradually, century by century, the Nile cut its way deeper down into the land, leaving banks of soil on either side between itself and the hills, and the mud which it brought down in its waters piled up at its mouth and pressed the sea back, till, at last, the Delta was formed, much as we see it now. This was long before Egypt had any story of its own; but even after history begins the Delta was still partly marshy land, not long reclaimed from the sea, and the real

Egyptians of the valley despised the people who lived there as mere marsh-dwellers. Even after the Delta was formed, the whole country was only about twice as large as Wales, and, though there was a great number of people in it for its size, the population was only, at the most, about twice as great as that of London.

An old Greek historian once said, "Egypt is the gift of the Nile," and it is perfectly true. We have seen how the great river made the country to begin with, cutting out the narrow valley through the hills, and building up the flat plain of the Delta. But the Nile has not only made the country; it keeps it alive. You know that Egypt has always been one of the most fertile lands in the world. Almost anything will grow there, and it produces wonderful crops of corn and vegetables, and, nowadays, of cotton. It was the same in old days. When Rome was the capital of the world, she used to get most of the corn to feed her hungry thousands from Egypt by the famous Alexandrian corn-ships; and you remember how, in the Bible story, Joseph's brethren came down from Palestine because, though there was famine there, there was "corn in Egypt." And yet Egypt is a land where rain is almost unknown. Sometimes there will come a heavy thunder-shower; but for month after month, year in and year out, there may be no rain at all.

How can a rainless country grow anything? The secret is the Nile. Every year, when the rains fall in the great lake-basin of Central Africa, from which one branch of the great river comes, and on the Abyssinian hills, where the other branch rises, the

Nile comes down in flood. All the lower lands are covered, and a fresh deposit of Nile mud is left upon them; and, though the river does not rise to the higher grounds, the water is led into big canals, and these, again, are divided up into little ones, till it circulates through the whole land, as the blood circulates through your arteries and veins. This keeps the land fertile, and makes up for the lack of rain.

Apart from its wonderful river, the country itself has no very striking features. It is rather a monotonous land--a long ribbon of green running through a great waste of yellow desert and barren hills. But the great charm that draws people's minds to Egypt, and gives the old land a never-failing interest, is its great story of the past, and all the relics of that story which are still to be seen.

In no other land can you see the real people and things of the days of long ago as you can see them in Egypt. Think how we should prize an actual building that had been connected with the story of King Arthur, if such a thing could be found in our country, and what wonderful romance would belong to the weapons, the actual shields and helmets, swords and lances, of the Knights of the Round Table, Lancelot and Tristram and Galahad--if only we could find them. Out there in Egypt you can see buildings compared with which King Arthur's Camelot would be only a thing of yesterday; and you can look, not only on the weapons, but on the actual faces and forms of great Kings and soldiers who lived, and fought bravely for their country, hundreds of years before Saul and Jonathan and

David began to fight the battles of Israel. You can see the pictures of how people lived in those far-away days, how their houses were built, how they traded and toiled, how they amused themselves, how they behaved in time of sorrow, how they worshipped God--all set down by themselves at the very time when they were doing these things. You can even see the games at which the children used to play, and the queer old-fashioned toys and dolls that they played with, and you can read the stories which their mothers and their nurses used to tell them.

These are the things which make this old land of Egypt so interesting to us all to-day; and I want to try to tell you about some of them, so that you may be able to have in your mind's eye a real picture of the life of those long past days.

CHAPTER II

A DAY IN THEBES

If any foreigner were wanting to get an idea of our country, and to see how our people live, I suppose the first place that he would go to would be London, because it is the capital of the whole country, and its greatest city; and so, if we want to learn something about Egypt, and how people lived there in those far-off days, we must try to get to the capital of the country, and see what is to be seen there.

Suppose, then, that we are no longer living in Britain in the twentieth century, but that somehow or other we have got away back into the past, far beyond the days of Jesus Christ, beyond even the times of Moses, and are living about 1,300 years before Christ. We have come from Tyre in a Phoenician galley, laden with costly bales of cloth dyed with Tyrian purple, and beautiful vessels wrought in bronze and copper, to sell in the markets of Thebes, the greatest city in Egypt. We have coasted along past Carmel and Joppa, and, after narrowly escaping being driven in a storm on the dangerous quicksand called the Syrtis, we have entered one of the mouths of the Nile. We have taken up an Egyptian pilot at the river mouth, and he stands on a little platform at the bow of the galley, and shouts his directions to the steersmen, who work the two big rudders, one on either side of the ship's stern. The north wind is blowing strongly and driving us swiftly upstream, in spite of the current of the great river; so our weary oarsmen have shipped their oars, and we drive steadily southwards under our one big swelling sail.

At first we sail along through a broad flat plain, partly cultivated, and partly covered with marsh and marsh plants. By-and-by the green plain begins to grow narrower; we are coming to the end of the Delta, and entering upon the real valley of Egypt. Soon we pass a great city, its temples standing out clear against the deep blue sky, with their towering gateways, gay flags floating from tall flagstaves in front of them, and great obelisks pointing to the sky; and our pilot says that this is Memphis, one of the oldest towns in the country, and for long its capital. Not far from Memphis, three great pyramid-shaped masses of stone rise up on the river-bank, looking almost like mountains; and the pilot tells us that these are the tombs of some of the great Kings of long past days, and that all around them lie smaller pyramids and other tombs of Kings and great men.

But we are bound for a city greater even than Memphis, and so we never stop, but hasten always southward. Several days of steady sailing carry us past many towns that cluster near the river, past one ruined city, falling into mere heaps of stone and brick, which our pilot tells us was once the capital of a wicked King who tried to cast down all the old gods of Egypt, and to set up a new god of his own; and at last we see, far ahead of us, a huge cluster of buildings on both sides of the river, which marks a city greater than we have ever seen.

As we sweep up the river we see that there are really two cities. On the east bank lies the city of the living, with its strong walls and towers, its enormous temples, and an endless crowd of houses of all sorts and sizes, from the gay palaces of the nobles to the mud huts of the poor people. On the west bank lies the city of the dead. It has neither streets nor palaces, and no hum of busy life goes up from it; but it is almost more striking than its neighbour across the river. The hills and cliffs are honeycombed with long rows of black openings, the doorways of the tombs where the dead of Thebes for centuries back are sleeping. Out on the plain, between the cliffs and the river, temple rises after temple in seemingly endless succession. Some of these temples are small and partly ruined, but some are very great and splendid; and, as the sunlight strikes upon them, it sends back flashes of gold and crimson and blue that dazzle the eyes.

But now our galley is drawing in towards the quay on the east side of the river, and in a few minutes the great sail comes thundering down, and, as the ship drifts slowly up to the quay, the mooring-ropes are thrown and made fast, and our long voyage is at an end. The Egyptian Custom-house officers come on board to examine the cargo, and collect the dues that have to be paid on it; and we watch them with interest, for they are quite different in appearance from our own hook-nosed, bearded sailors, with their thick many-coloured cloaks. These Egyptians are all clean shaven; some of them wear wigs, and some have their hair cut straight across their brows, while it falls thickly behind upon their necks in a multitude of little curls, which must have taken them no small trouble to get into order. Most wear nothing but a kilt of white linen; but the chief officer has a fine white cloak thrown over his shoulders; his linen kilt is stiffly starched, so that it stands out almost like a board where it folds over in front, and he wears a gilded girdle with fringed ends which hang down nearly to his knees. In his right hand he carries a long stick, which he is not slow to lay over the shoulders of his men when they do not obey his orders fast enough.

After a good deal of hot argument, the amount of the tax is settled and paid, and we are free to go up into the great town. We have not gone far before we find that life in Thebes can be quite exciting. A

great noise is heard from one of the narrow
riverside streets, and a crowd of men comes rushing
up with shouts and oaths. Ahead of them runs a
single figure, whose writing-case, stuck in his
girdle, marks him out as a scribe. He is almost at his
last gasp, for he is stout and not accustomed to
running; and he is evidently fleeing for his life, for
the men behind him--rough, half-naked, ill-fed
creatures of the working class--are chasing him
with cries of anger, and a good deal of stone-
throwing. Bruised and bleeding, he darts up to the
gate of a handsome house whose garden-wall faces
the street. He gasps out a word to the porter, and is
quickly passed into the garden. The gate is slammed
and bolted in the faces of his pursuers, who form a
ring round it, shouting and shaking their fists.

In a little while the gate is cautiously unbarred, and
a fine-looking man, very richly dressed, and
followed by half a dozen well-armed negro guards,
steps forward, and asks the workmen why they are
here, making such a noise, and why they have
chased and beaten his secretary. He is Prince Paser,
who has charge of the Works Department of the
Theban Government, and the workmen are masons
employed on a large job in the cemetery of Thebes.
They all shout at once in answer to the Prince's
question; but by-and-by they push forward a
spokesman, and he begins, rather sheepishly at first,
but warming up as he goes along, to make their
complaint to the great man.

He and his mates, he says, have been working for
weeks. They have had no wages; they have not even
had the corn and oil which ought to be issued as

rations to Government workmen. So they have struck work, and now they have come to their lord the Prince to entreat him either to give command that the rations be issued, or, if his stores are exhausted, to appeal to Pharaoh. "We have been driven here by hunger and thirst; we have no clothes, we have no oil, we have no food. Write to our lord the Pharaoh, that he may give us something for our sustenance." When the spokesman has finished his complaint, the whole crowd volubly assents to what he has said, and sways to and fro in a very threatening manner.

Prince Paser, however, is an old hand at dealing with such complaints. With a smiling face he promises that fifty sacks of corn shall be sent to the cemetery immediately, with oil to correspond. Only the workmen must go back to their work at once, and there must be no more chasing of poor Secretary Amen-nachtu. Otherwise, he can do nothing. The workmen grumble a little. They have been put off with promises before, and have got little good of them. But they have no leader bold enough to start a riot, and they have no weapons, and the spears and bows of the Prince's Nubians look dangerous. Finally they turn, and disappear, grumbling, down the street from which they came; and Prince Paser, with a shrug of his shoulders, goes indoors again. Whether the fifty sacks of corn are ever sent or not, is another matter. Strikes, you see, were not unknown, even so long ago as this.

CHAPTER III

A DAY IN THEBES--Continued

Having seen the settlement of the masons' strike, we wander up into the heart of the town. The streets are generally narrow and winding, and here and there the houses actually meet overhead, so that we pass out of the blinding sunlight into a sort of dark tunnel. Some of the houses are large and high; but even the largest make no display towards the street. They will be fine enough inside, with bright courts surrounded with trees, in the midst of which lies a cool pond of water, and with fine rooms decorated with gay hangings; but their outer walls are almost absolutely blank, with nothing but a heavy door breaking the dead line. We pass by some quarters where there is nothing but a crowd of mud huts, packed so closely together that there is only room for a single foot-passenger to thread his way through the narrow alleys between them. These are the workmen's quarters, and the heat and smell in them are so overpowering that one wonders how people can live in such places.

By-and-by we come out into a more open space-- one of the bazaars of the city--where business is in full swing. The shops are little shallow booths quite open to the front; and all the goods are spread out round the shopkeeper, who squats cross-legged in the middle of his property, ready to serve his customers, and invites the attention of the passers-by by loud explanations of the goodness and cheapness of his wares. All sorts of people are coming and going, for a Theban crowd holds representatives of nearly every nation known. Here are the townsfolk, men and women, out to buy supplies for their houses, or to exchange the news of the day; peasants from the villages round about, bringing in vegetables and cattle to barter for the goods which can only be got in the town; fine ladies and gentlemen, dressed elaborately in the latest Court fashion, with carefully curled wigs, long pleated robes of fine transparent linen, and dainty, brightly-coloured sandals turned up at the toes. At one moment you rub shoulders with a Hittite from Kadesh, a conspicuous figure, with his high-peaked cap, pale complexion, and heavy, pointed boots. He looks round him curiously, as if thinking that Thebes would be a splendid town to plunder. Then a priest of high rank goes by, with shaven head, a panther skin slung across his shoulder over his white robe, and a roll of papyrus in his hand. A Sardinian of the bodyguard swaggers along behind him, the ball and horns on his helmet flashing in the sunlight, his big sword swinging in its sheath as he walks; and a Libyan bowman, with two bright feathers in his leather skull-cap, looks disdainfully at him as he shoulders his way through the crowd.

All around us people are buying and selling. Money, as we know it, has not yet been invented, and nearly all the trade is done by means of exchange. When it comes to be a question of how many fish have to be given for a bed, or whether a load of onions is good value for a chair, you can imagine that there has to be a good deal of argument. Besides, the Egyptian dearly loves bargaining for the mere excitement of the thing, and so the clatter of tongues is deafening. Here and there one or two traders have advanced a little beyond the old-fashioned way of barter, and offer, instead of goods, so many rings of copper, silver, or gold wire. A peasant who has brought in a bullock to sell is offered 90 copper "uten" (as the rings are called) for it; but he loudly protests that this is robbery, and after a long argument he screws the merchant up to 111 "uten," with 8 more as a luck-penny, and the bargain is clinched. Even then the rings have still to be weighed that he may be sure he is not being cheated. So a big pair of balances is brought out; the "uten" are heaped into one scale, and in the other are piled weights in the shape of bulls' heads. Finally, he is satisfied, and picks up his bag of rings; but the wily merchant is not done with him yet. He spreads out various tempting bargains before the eyes of the countryman, and, before the latter leaves the shop, most of the copper rings have found their way back again to the merchant's sack.

A little farther on, the Tyrian traders, to whom the cargo of our galley is consigned, have their shop. Screens, made of woven grass, shelter it from the sun, and under their shade all sorts of gorgeous stuffs are displayed, glowing with the deep rich colours, of which the Tyrians alone have the secret since the sack of Knossos destroyed the trade of Crete. Beyond the Tyrian booth, a goldsmith is busily employed in his shop. Necklets and bracelets of gold and silver, beautifully inlaid with all kinds of rich colours, hang round him; and he is hard at work, with his little furnace and blowpipe, putting the last touches to the welding of a bracelet, for which a lady is patiently waiting.

In one corner of the bazaar stands a house which makes no display of wares, but, nevertheless, seems to secure a constant stream of customers. Workmen slink in at the door, as though half ashamed of themselves, and reappear, after a little, wiping their mouths, and not quite steady in their gait. A young man, with pale and haggard face, swaggers past and goes in, and, as he enters the door, one bystander nudges another and remarks: "Pentuere is going to have a good day again; he will come to a bad end, that young man."

By-and-by the door opens again, and Pentuere comes out staggering. He looks vacantly round, and tries to walk away; but his legs refuse to carry him, and, after a stumble or two, he falls in a heap and lies in the road, a pitiful sight. The passers-by jeer and laugh at him as he lies helpless; but one decent-looking man points him out to his young son, and says: "See this fellow, my son, and learn not to drink beer to excess. Thou dost fall and break thy limbs, and bespatter thyself with mud, like a crocodile, and no one reaches out a hand to thee. Thy comrades go on drinking, and say, 'Away with this fellow, who is drunk.' If anyone should seek thee on business, thou art found lying in the dust like a little child."

But in spite of much wise advice, the Egyptian, though generally temperate, is only too fond of making "a good day," as he calls it, at the beerhouse. Even fine ladies sometimes drink too much at their great parties, and have to be carried away very sick and miserable. Worst of all, the very judges of the High Court have been known to take a day off during the hearing of a long case, in order to have a revel with the criminals whom they were trying; and it is not so long since two of them had their noses cut off, as a warning to the rest against such shameful conduct.

Sauntering onwards, we gradually get near to the sacred quarter of the town, and can see the towering gateways and obelisks of the great temples over the roofs of the houses. Soon a great crowd comes towards us, and the sounds of trumpets and flutes are heard coming from the midst of it. Inquiring what is the meaning of the bustle, we are told that one of the images of Amen, the great god of Thebes, is being carried in procession as a preliminary to an important service which is to take place in the afternoon, and at which the King is going to preside. Stepping back under the doorway of a house, we watch the procession go past. After a group of musicians and singers, and a number of women who are dancing as they go, and shaking curious metal rattles, there comes a group of six men, who form the centre of the whole crowd, and on whom the eyes of all are fixed.

They are tall, spare, keen-looking men, their heads clean shaven, their bodies wrapped in pure white robes of the beautiful Egyptian linen. On their shoulders they carry, by means of two long poles, a model of a Nile boat, in the midst of which rises a little shrine. The shrine is carefully draped round with a veil, so as to hide the god from curious eyes. But just in front of the doorway where we are standing a small stone pillar rises from the roadway, and when the bearers come to this point, the bark of

the god is rested on the top of the pillar. Two
censer-bearers come forward, and swing their
censers, wafting clouds of incense round the shrine;
a priest lifts up his voice, loudly intoning a hymn of
praise to the great god who creates and sustains all
things; and a few of the by-standers lay before the
bark offerings of flowers, fruit, and eatables of
various kinds. Then comes the solemn moment.
Amid breathless silence, the veil of the shrine is
slowly drawn aside, and the faithful can see a little
wooden image, about 18 inches high, adorned with
tall plumes, carefully dressed, and painted with
green and black. The revelation of this little doll, to
a Theban crowd the most sacred object in all the
world, is hailed with shouts of wonder and
reverence. Then the veil is drawn again, the
procession passes on, and the streets are left quiet
for awhile.

We are reminded that, if we wish to get a meal
before starting out to see Pharaoh passing in
procession to the temple, we had better lose no
time, and so we turn our faces riverwards again, and
wander down through the endless maze of streets to
where our galley is moored at the quay.

CHAPTER IV

PHARAOH AT HOME

The time is coming on now for the King to go in
state to the great temple at Karnak to offer sacrifice,

and as we go up to the palace to see him come forth in all his glory, let me tell you a little about him and the kind of life he leads. Pharaoh, of course, is not his real name; it is not even his official title; it is just a word which is used to describe a person who is so great that people scarcely venture to call him by his proper name. Just as the Turks nowadays speak of the "Sublime Porte," when they mean the Sultan and his Government, so the Egyptians speak of "Per-o," or Pharaoh, as we call it, which really signifies "Great House," when they mean the King.

For the King of Egypt is a very great man indeed; in fact, his people look upon him, and he looks upon himself, as something more than a man. There are many gods in Egypt; but the god whom the people know best, and to whom they pay the most reverence, is their King. Ever since there have been Kings in the country, and that is a very long time now, the reigning monarch has been looked upon as a kind of god manifest in the flesh. He calls himself "Son of the Sun"; in the temples you will see pictures of his childhood, where great goddesses dandle the young god upon their knees. Divine honours are paid, and sacrifices offered to him; and when he dies, and goes to join his brother-gods in heaven, a great temple rises to his memory, and hosts of priests are employed in his worship. There is just one distinction made between him and the other gods. Amen at Thebes, Ptah at Memphis, and all the rest of the crowd of divinities, are called "the great gods." Pharaoh takes a different title. He is called "the good god."

At present "the good god" is Ramses II. Of course,

that is only one part of his name; for, like all the other Pharaohs, he has a list of titles that would fill a page. His subjects in Thebes have not seen very much of him for a long time, for there has been so much to do away in Syria, that he has built another capital at Tanis, which the Hebrews call Zoan, down between the Delta and the eastern frontier, and spends most of his time there. People who have been down the river tell us great wonders about the beauty of the new town, its great temple, and the huge statue of the King, 90 feet high, which stands before the temple gate. But Thebes is still the centre of the nation's life, and now, when it is growing almost certain that there will be another war with those vile Hittites in the North of Syria, he has come up to the great city to take counsel with his brother-god, Amen, and to make arrangements for gathering his army. The royal palace is in a constant bustle, with envoys coming and going, and counsellors and generals continually passing in and out with reports and orders.

Outside, the palace is not so very imposing. The Egyptians built their temples to last for ever; but the palaces of their Kings were meant to serve only for a short time. The new King might not care for the old King's home, and so each Pharaoh builds his house according to his own taste, of light materials. It will serve his turn, and his successor may build another for himself. A high wall, with battlements, towers, and heavy gates, surrounds it; for, though Pharaoh is a god, his subjects are sometimes rather difficult to keep in order. Plots against the King have not been unknown in the past; and on at least one occasion, a great Pharaoh of bygone days had to spring from his couch and fight single-handed for his life against a crowd of conspirators who had forced an entrance into the palace while he was enjoying his siesta. So since then Pharaoh has found it better to trust in his strong walls, and in the big broadswords of his faithful Sardinian guardsmen, than in any divinity that may belong to himself.

Within the great boundary wall lie pleasant gardens, gay with all sorts of flowers, and an artificial lake shows its gleaming water here and there through the trees and shrubs. The palace itself is all glittering white stucco on the outside. A high central door leads into a great audience hall, glowing with colour, its roof supported by painted pillars in the form of lotus-stalks; and on either side of this lie two smaller halls. Behind the audience chamber are two immense dining-rooms, and behind these come the sleeping apartments of the numerous household. Ramses has a multitude of wives, and a whole army of sons and daughters, and it takes no small space to house them all. The bedroom of the great King himself stands apart from the other rooms, and is surrounded by banks of flowers in full bloom.

The Son of the Sun has had a busy day already. He has had many letters and despatches to read and consider. Some of the Syrian vassal-princes have sent clay tablets, covered with their curious arrow-headed writing, giving news of the advance of the Hittites, and imploring the help of the Egyptian army; and now the King is about to give audience, and to consider these with his great nobles and Generals. At one end of the reception hall stands a low balcony, supported on gaily-painted wooden pillars which end in capitals of lotus-flowers. The front of this balcony is overlaid with gold, and richly decorated with turquoise and lapis lazuli. Here the King will show himself to his subjects, accompanied by his favourite wife, Queen Nefertari, and some of the young Princes and Princesses. The folding doors of the audience chamber are thrown open, and the barons, the provincial governors, and the high officers of the army and the State throng in to do homage to their master.

In a few moments the glittering crowd is duly arranged, a door opens at the back of the balcony, and the King of the Two Lands, Lord of the Vulture and the Snake, steps forth with his Queen and family. In earlier times, whenever the King appeared, the assembled nobles were expected to fall on their faces and kiss the ground before him. Fashion has changed, however, and now the great folks, at all events, are no longer required to "smell the earth." As Pharaoh enters the balcony, the nobles bow profoundly, and raise their arms as if in prayer to "the good god." Then, in silent reverence, they wait until it shall please their lord to speak.

Ramses sweeps his glance over the crowd, singles out the General in command of the Theban troops, and puts a question to him as to the readiness of his division--the picked division of the army. The soldier steps forward with a deep bow; but it is not Court manners for him to answer his lord's question directly. Instead, he begins by reciting a little psalm of praise, which tells of the King's greatness, his valour and skill in war, and asserts that wherever his horses tread his enemies flee before him and perish. This little piece of flattery over, the General begins, "O King, my master," and in a few sensible words gives the information required. So the audience goes on, counsellor after counsellor coming forward at the royal command, reciting his little hymn, and then giving his opinion on such matters as his master suggests to him. At last the council is over, the King gives orders to his equerry to prepare his chariot for the procession to the temple, and, as he turns to leave the audience chamber, the assembled nobles once more bow profoundly, and raise their arms in adoration.

After a short delay, the great gates of the boundary wall of the palace are opened; a company of spearmen, in quilted leather kilts and leather skull-caps, marches out, and takes position a short distance from the gateway. Behind them comes a company of the Sardinians of the guard, heavily armed, with bright helmets, broad round shields, quilted corselets, and long, heavy, two-edged swords. They range themselves on either side of the roadway, and stand like statues, waiting for the appearance of Pharaoh. There is a whir of chariot-wheels, and the royal chariot sweeps through the gateway, and sets off at a good round pace towards the temple. The spearmen in front start at the double, and the guardsmen, in spite of their heavy equipment, keep pace with their royal master on either side.

The waiting crowd bows to the dust as the sovereign passes; but Pharaoh looks neither to the right hand nor to the left. He stands erect and impassive in the swaying chariot, holding the crook and whip which are the Egyptian royal emblems. On his head he wears the royal war helmet, in the front of which a golden cobra rears its crest from its coils, as if to threaten the enemies of Egypt. His finely-shaped, swarthy features are adorned, or disfigured, by an artificial beard, which is fastened on by a strap passing up in front of the ears. His tall slender body is covered, above his corselet, with a robe of fine white linen, a perfect wonder of pleating; and round his waist passes a girdle of gold and green enamel, whose ends cross and hang down almost to his knees, terminating in two threatening cobra heads. On either side of him run the fan-bearers, who manage, by a miracle of skill and activity, to keep their great gaily-coloured fans of perfumed ostrich feathers waving round the royal head even as they run.

Behind the King comes a long train of other chariots, only less splendid than that of Ramses. In the first stands Queen Nefertari, languidly sniffing at a lotus-flower as she passes on. The others are filled by some of the Princes of the blood, who are going to take part in the ceremony at the temple, chief among them the wizard Prince Khaemuas, the greatest magician in Egypt, who has spells that can bring the dead from their graves. Some in the crowd shrink from his keen eye, and mutter that the papyrus roll which he holds so close to his breast was taken from the grave of another magician Prince of ancient days, and that Khaemuas will know no peace till it is restored. In a few minutes the whole brilliant train has passed, dazzling the eyes with a blaze of gold and white and scarlet; and crowds of courtiers stream after their master, as fast as their feet can carry them, towards Karnak. You have seen, if only for a moment, the greatest man on earth--the Great Oppressor of Hebrew story. Very mighty and very proud he is; and he does not dream that the little Hebrew boy whom his daughter has adopted, and who is being trained in the priestly college at Heliopolis, will one day humble all the pride of Egypt, and that the very name of Ramses shall be best remembered because it is linked with that of Moses.

CHAPTER V

THE LIFE OF A SOLDIER

When you read about the Egyptians in the Bible, it seems as though they were nearly always fighting; and, indeed, they did a good deal of fighting in their time, as nearly every nation did in those old days. But in reality they were not a great soldier people, like their rivals the Assyrians, or the Babylonians. We, who have had so much to do with their descendants, the modern Egyptians, and have fought both against them and with them, know that the "Gippy" is not fond of soldiering in his heart. He makes a very good, patient, hardworking soldier when he has good officers; but he is not like the Soudanese, who love fighting for fighting's sake. He much prefers to live quietly in his own native village, and cultivate his own bit of ground. And his forefathers, in these long-past days, were very much of the same mind. Often, of course, they had to fight, when Pharaoh ordered them out for a campaign in the Soudan or in Syria, and then they fought wonderfully well; but all the time their hearts were at home, and they were glad to get back to their farm-work and their simple pleasures. They were a peaceful, kindly, pleasant race, with little of the cruelty and fierceness that you find continually among the Assyrians.

In fact, the old Egyptian rather despised soldiering as a profession. He thought it was rather a miserable, muddled kind of a job, in which, unless you were a great officer, you got all the hard knocks and none of the honours; and I am not sure that he was far wrong. His great idea of a happy life was to get employment as a scribe, or, as we should say, a clerk, to some big man or to the Government, to keep accounts and write reports. Of course the people could not all be scribes; but an Egyptian who had sons was never so proud as when he could get one of them into a scribe's position, even though the young man might look down upon his old father and his brothers, toiling on the land or serving in the army.

A curious old book has come down to us from these ancient days, in which the writer, who had been both a soldier and a high officer under Government in what we should call the diplomatic service, has told a young friend his opinion of soldiering as a profession. The young man had evidently been dazzled with the idea of being in the cavalry, or, rather, the chariotry, for the Egyptian soldiers did not ride on horses like our cavalry, but drove them in chariots, in each of which there were two men--

the charioteer, to drive the two horses, and the soldier, who stood beside the driver and fought with the bow, and sometimes with the lance or sword.

But this wise old friend tells him that even to be in the chariotry is not by any means a pleasant job. Of course it seems very nice at first. The young man gets his new equipment, and thinks all the world of himself as he goes home to show off his fine feathers.

"He receives beautiful horses, And rejoices and exults, And returns with them to his town."

But then comes the inspection, and if he has not everything in perfect order he has a bad time of it, for he is thrown down on the ground, and beaten with sticks till he is sore all over.

But if the lot of the cavalry soldier is hard, that of the infantry-man is harder. In the barracks he is flogged for every mistake or offence. Then war breaks out, and he has to march with his battalion to Syria. Day after day he has to tramp on foot through the wild hill-country, so different from the flat, fertile homeland that he loves. He has to carry all his heavy equipment and his rations, so that he is laden like a donkey; and often he has to drink dirty water, which makes him ill. Then, when the battle comes, he gets all the danger and the wounds, while the Generals get all the credit. When the war is over, he comes home riding on a donkey, a broken-down man, sick and wounded, his very clothes stolen by the rascals who should have attended on him. Far better, the wise man says, to be a scribe, and to remain comfortably at home. I dare say it was all quite true, just as perhaps it would not be very far from the truth at the present time; but, in spite of it all, Pharaoh had his battles to fight, and he got his soldiers all right when they were needed.

The Egyptian army was not generally a very big one. It was nothing like the great hosts that we hear of nowadays, or read of in some of the old histories. The armies that the Pharaohs led into Syria were not often much bigger than what we should call an army corps nowadays--probably about 20,000 men altogether, rarely more than 25,000. But in that number you could find almost as many different sorts of men as in our own Indian army. There would be first the native Egyptian spearmen and bowmen--the spearmen with leather caps and quilted leather tunics, carrying a shield and spear, and sometimes an axe, or a dagger, or short sword-- the bowmen, more lightly equipped, but probably more dangerous enemies, for the Egyptian archers were almost as famous as the old English bowmen, and won many a battle for their King. Then came the chariot brigade, also of native Egyptians, men probably of higher rank than the foot-soldiers. The chariots were very light, and it must have been exceedingly difficult for the bowman to balance himself in the narrow car, as it bumped and clattered over rough ground. The two horses were gaily decorated, and often wore plumes on their heads. The charioteer sometimes twisted the reins round his waist, and could take a hand in the fighting if his companion was hard pressed, guiding his horses by swaying his body to one side or the other.

Round the Pharaoh himself, as he stood in his beautiful chariot, marched the royal bodyguard. It was made up of men whom the Egyptians called "Sherden"--Sardinians, probably, who had come over the sea to serve for hire in the army of the great King. They wore metal helmets, with a round ball on the top and horns at the sides, carried round bossed shields, and were armed with great heavy swords of much the same shape as those which the Norman knights used to carry. Behind the native troops and the bodyguard marched the other mercenaries--regiments of black Soudanese, with wild-beast skins thrown over their ebony shoulders; and light-coloured Libyans from the West, each with a couple of feathers stuck in his leather skull-cap.

Scouts went on ahead to scour the country, and bring to the King reports of the enemy's whereabouts. Beside the royal chariot there padded along a strange, but very useful soldier--a great tame lion, which had been trained to guard his master and fight with teeth and claws against his enemies. Last of all came the transport train, with the baggage carried on the backs of a long line of donkeys, and protected by a baggage-guard. The Egyptians were good marchers, and even in the hot Syrian sunshine, and across a rough country where roads were almost unknown, they could keep up a steady fifteen miles a day for a week on end without being fagged out.

Let us follow the fortunes of an Egyptian soldier through one of the great battles of the nation's history. Menna was one of the most skilful charioteers of the whole Egyptian army--so skilful that, though he was still quite young, he was promoted to be driver of the royal war-chariot when King Ramses II. marched out from Zaru, the frontier garrison town of Egypt, to fight with the Hittites in Northern Syria. During all the long march across the desert, through Palestine, and over the northern mountain passes, no enemy was seen at all, and, though Menna was kept busy enough attending to his horses and seeing that the chariot was in perfect order, he was in no danger. But as the army began to wind down the long valley of the Orontes towards the town of Kadesh, the scouts were kept out in every direction, and the whole host was anxiously on the lookout for the Hittite troops.

Kadesh came in sight at last. Far on the horizon its towers could be seen, and the sun's rays sparkled on the river and on the broad moat which surrounded the walls; but still no enemy was to be seen. The scouts came in with the report that the Hittites had retreated northwards in terror, and King Ramses imagined that Kadesh was going to fall into his hands without a battle. His army was divided into four brigades, and he himself hurried on rather rashly with the first brigade, leaving the other three to straggle on behind him, widely separated from one another.

The first brigade reached its camping-ground to the north-west of Kadesh; the tired troops pitched camp; the baggage was unloaded; and the donkeys, released from their burdens, rolled on the ground in delight. Just at that moment some of the Egyptian scouts came in, bringing with them two Arabs whom they had caught, and suspected to belong to the enemy. King Ramses ordered the Arabs to be soundly beaten with sticks, and the poor creatures confessed that the Hittite King, with a great army, was concealed on the other side of Kadesh, watching for an opportunity to attack the Egyptian army. In great haste Ramses, scolding his scouts the while for not keeping a better lookout, began to get his soldiers under arms again, while Menna ran and yoked to the royal chariot the two noble horses which had been kept fresh for the day of battle.

But before Pharaoh could leap into his chariot a wild uproar broke out at the gate of the camp, and the scattered fragments of the second brigade came pouring in headlong flight into the enclosure. Behind them the whole Hittite chariot force, 2,500 chariots strong, each chariot with three men in it, came clattering and leaping upon the heels of the fugitives. The Hittite King had waited till he saw the first brigade busy pitching camp, and then, as the second came straggling up, he had launched his chariots upon the flank of the weary soldiers, who were swept away in a moment as if by a flood.

The rush of terrified men carried off the first brigade along with it in hopeless rout. Ramses and Menna were left with only a few picked chariots of the household troops, and the whole Hittite army was coming on. But though King Ramses had made a terrible bungle of his generalship, he was at least a brave man. Leaping into his chariot, and calling to the handful of faithful soldiers to follow him, he bade Menna lash his horses and charge the advancing Hittites. Menna was no coward, but when he saw the thin line of Egyptian troops, and looked at the dense mass of Hittite chariots, his heart almost failed him. He never thought of disobedience, but, as he stooped over his plunging horses, he panted to the King: "O mighty strength of Egypt in the day of battle, we are alone in the midst of the enemy. O, save us, Ramses, my good lord!" "Steady, steady, my charioteer," said Ramses, "I am going among them like a hawk!"

In a moment the fiery horses were whirling the King and his charioteer between the files of the Hittite chariots, which drew aside as if terrified at the glittering figures that dashed upon them so fearlessly. As they swept through, Menna had enough to do to manage his steeds, which were wild with excitement; but Ramses' bow was bent again and again, and at every twang of the bowstring a Hittite champion fell from his chariot. Behind the King came his household troops, and all together they burst through the chariot brigade of the enemy, leaving a long trail marked by dead and wounded men, overturned chariots, and maddened horses.

Still King Ramses had only gained a breathing-space. The Hittites far outnumbered his little force, and, though his orderlies were madly galloping to bring up the third and fourth brigades, it must be some time yet before even the nearest could come into action. Besides, on the other bank of the river there hung a great cloud of 8,000 Hittite spearmen, under the command of the Hittite King himself. If these got time to cross the river, the Egyptian position, bad enough as it was, would be hopeless. There was nothing for it but to charge again and

again, and, if possible, drive back the Hittite
chariots on the river, so as to hinder the spearmen
from crossing.

So Menna whipped up his horses again, and, with
arrow on string, the Pharaoh dashed upon his
enemies once more. Again they burst through the
opposing ranks, scattering death on either side as
they passed. Now some of the fragments of the first
and second brigades were beginning to rally and
come back to the field, and the struggle was
becoming less unequal. The Egyptian quivers were
nearly all empty now; but lance and sword still
remained, and inch by inch the Hittites were forced
back upon the river. Their King stood ingloriously
on the opposite bank, unable to do anything. It was
too late for him to try to move his spearmen across--
they would only have been trampled down by the
retreating chariots. At last a great shout from the
rear announced the arrival of the third Egyptian
brigade, and, the little knot of brave men who had
saved the day still leading, the army swept the
broken Hittites down the bank of the Orontes into
the river.

Great was the confusion and the slaughter. As the
chariots struggled through the ford, the Egyptian
bowmen, spread out along the bank, picked off the
chiefs. The two brothers of the Hittite King, the
chief of his bodyguard, his shield-bearer, and his
chief scribe, were all killed. The King of Aleppo
missed the ford, and was swept down the river; but
some of his soldiers dashed into the water, rescued
him, and, in rough first aid, held the half-drowned
leader up by the heels, to let the water drain out of

him. The Hittite King picked up his broken fugitives, covered them with his mass of spearmen, and moved reluctantly off the field where so splendid a chance of victory had been missed, and turned into defeat. The Egyptians were too few and too weary to attempt to cross the river in pursuit, and they retired to the camp of the first brigade.

Then Pharaoh called his Captains before him. The troops stood around, leaning on their spears, ashamed of their conduct in the earlier part of the day, and wondering at the grim signs of conflict that lay on every side. King Ramses called Menna to him, and, handing the reins to a groom, the young charioteer came bowing before his master. Pharaoh stripped from his own royal neck a collar of gold, and fastened it round the neck of his faithful squire; and, while the Generals and Captains hung their heads for shame, the King told them how shamefully they had left him to fight his battle alone, and how none had stood by him but the young charioteer. "As for my two horses," he said, "they shall be fed before me every day in the royal palace."

Both armies had suffered too much loss for any further strife to be possible, and a truce was agreed upon. The Hittites drew off to the north, and the Egyptians marched back again to Egypt, well aware that they had gained little or nothing by all their efforts, but thankful that they had been saved from the total destruction which had seemed so near.

A proud man was Menna when he drove the royal chariot up to the bridge of Zaru. As the troops passed the frontier canal the road was lined on either side with crowds of nobles, priests, and scribes, strewing flowers in the way, and bowing before the King. And after the Pharaoh himself, whose bravery had saved the day, there was no one so honoured as the young squire who had stood so manfully by his master in the hour of danger.

CHAPTER VI

CHILD-LIFE IN ANCIENT EGYPT

How did the boys and girls live in this quaint old land so many hundreds of years ago? How were they dressed, what sort of games did they play at, what sort of lessons did they learn, and what kind of school did they go to? If you could have lived in Egypt in those far-off days, you would have found many differences between your life of to-day and the life that the Egyptian children led; but you would also have found that there were very many things much the same then as they are now. Boys and girls were boys and girls three thousand years ago, just as they are now; and you would find that they did very much the same things, and even played very much the same games as you do to-day.

When you read in your fairy-stories about a little boy or girl, you often hear that they had fairy godmothers who came to their cradles, and gave them gifts, and foretold what was going to happen to the little babies in after years. Well, when little

Tahuti or little Sen-senb was born in Thebes fifteen hundred years before Christ, there were fairy godmothers too, who presided over the great event; and there were others called the Hathors, who foretold all that was going to happen to the little boy or girl as the years went on. The baby was kept a baby much longer in those days than our little ones are kept. The happy mother nursed the little thing carefully for three years at all events, carrying it about with her wherever she went, either on her shoulder, or astride upon her hip.

If baby took ill, and the doctor was called in, the medicines that were given were not in the least like the sugar-coated pills and capsules that make medicine-taking easy nowadays. The Egyptian doctor did not know a very great deal about medicine and sickness, but he made up for his ignorance by the nastiness of the doses which he gave to his patients. I don't think you would like to take pills made up of the moisture scraped from pig's ears, lizard's blood, bad meat, and decaying fat, to say nothing of still nastier things. Often the doctor would look very grave, and say, "The child is not ill; he is bewitched"; and then he would sit down and write out a prescription something like this: "Remedy to drive away bewitchment. Take a great beetle; cut off his head and his wings, boil him, put him in oil, and lay him out. Then cook his head and his wings; put them in snake-fat, boil, and let the patient drink the mixture." I think you would almost rather take the risk of being bewitched than drink a dose like that!

Sometimes the doctor gave no medicines at all, but

wrote a few magic words on a scrap of old paper, and tied it round the part where the pain was. I daresay it did as much good as his pills. Very often the mother believed that it was not really sickness that was troubling her child, but that a ghost was coming and hurting him; so when his cries showed that the ghost was in the room, the mother would rise up, shaking all over, I daresay, and would repeat the verse that she had been taught would drive ghosts away:

"Comest thou to kiss this child? I suffer thee not to kiss him; Comest thou to quiet him? I suffer thee not to quiet him; Comest thou to harm him? I suffer thee not to harm him; Comest thou to take him away? I suffer thee not to take him away."

When little Tahuti has got over his baby aches, and escaped the ghosts, he begins to run about and play. He and his sister are not bothered to any great extent with dressing in the mornings. They are very particular about washing, but as Egypt is so hot, clothes are not needed very much, and so the little boy and girl play about with nothing at all on their little brown bodies except, perhaps, a narrow girdle, or even a single thread tied round the waist. They have their toys just like you. Tahuti has got a wonderful man, who, when you pull a string, works a roller up and down upon a board, just like a baker rolling out dough, and besides he has a crocodile that moves its jaws. His sister has dolls: a fine Egyptian lady and a frizzy-haired, black-faced Nubian girl. Sometimes they play together at ninepins, rolling the ball through a little gate.

For about four years this would go on, as long as Tahuti was what the Egyptians called "a wise little one." Then, when he was four years old, the time came when he had to become "a writer in the house of books," which is what the Egyptians called a school-boy; so little Tahuti set off for school, still wearing no more clothes than the thread tied round his waist, and with his black hair plaited up into a long thick lock, which hung down over his right ear. The first thing that he had to learn was how to read and write, and this was no easy task, for Egyptian writing, though it is very beautiful when well done, is rather difficult to master, all the more as there were two different styles which had to be learned if a boy was going to become a man of learning. I don't suppose that you think your old copy-books of much importance when you are done with them; but the curious thing is that among all the books that have come down to us from ancient Egypt, there are far more old copy-books than any others, and these books, with the teachers' corrections written on the margins, and rough sketches scratched in here and there among the writing, have proved most valuable in telling us what the Egyptians learned, and what they liked to read; for a great deal of the writing consisted in the copying out of wise words of the men of former days, and sometimes of stories of old times.

These old copy-books can speak to us in one way, but if they could speak in another, I daresay they would tell us of many weary hours in school, and of many floggings and tears; for the Egyptian school-master believed with all his heart in the cane, and used it with great vigour and as often as he could.

Little Tahuti used to look forward to his daily flogging, much as he did to his lunch in the middle of the day, when his careful mother regularly brought him three rolls of bread and two jugs of beer. "A boy's ears," his master used to say, "are on his back, and he hears when he is beaten." One of the former pupils at his school writing to his teacher, and recalling his school-days, says: "I was with thee since I was brought up as a child; thou didst beat my back, and thine instructions went into my ear." Sometimes the boys, if they were stubborn, got punishments even worse than the cane. Another boy, in a letter to his old master, says: "Thou hast made me buckle to since the time that I was one of thy pupils. I spent my time in the lock-up, and was sentenced to three months, and bound in the temple." I am afraid our schoolboys would think the old Egyptian teachers rather more severe than the masters with whom they have to do nowadays.

Lesson-time occupied about half the day, and when it came to an end the boys all ran out of the school, shouting for joy. That custom has not changed much, anyway, in all these hundreds of years. I don't think they had any home lessons to do, and so, perhaps, their school-time was not quite so bad as we might imagine from the rough punishments they used to get.

When Tahuti grew a little older, and had fairly mastered the rudiments of writing, his teacher set him to write out copies of different passages from the best known Egyptian books, partly to keep up his hand-writing, and partly to teach him to know good Egyptian and to use correct language.

Sometimes it was a piece of a religious book that he was set to copy, sometimes a poem, sometimes a fairy-tale. For the Egyptians were very fond of fairy-tales, and later on, perhaps, we may hear some of their stories, the oldest fairy-stories in the world. But generally the piece that was chosen was one which would not only exercise the boy's hand, and teach him a good style, but would also help to teach him good manners, and fill his mind with right ideas. Very often Tahuti's teacher would dictate to him a passage from the wise advice which a great King of long ago left to his son, the Crown Prince, or from some other book of the same kind. And sometimes the exercises would be in the form of letters which the master and his pupils wrote as though they had been friends far away from one another. Tahuti's letters, you may be sure, were full of wisdom and of good resolutions, and I dare say he was just about as fond of writing them as you are of writing the letters that your teacher sometimes sets as a task for you.

When it came to Arithmetic, Tahuti was so far lucky that the number of rules he had to learn was very few. His master taught him addition and subtraction, and a very slow and clumsy form of multiplication; but he could not teach him division, for the very simple reason that he did not properly understand it himself. Enough of mensuration was taught him to enable him to find out, though rather roughly, what was the size of a field, and how much corn would go into a granary of any particular size. And when he had learned these things, his elementary education was pretty well over.

Of course a great deal would depend on the profession he was going to follow. If he was going to be only a common scribe, his education would go no farther; for the work he would have to do would need no greater learning than reading, writing, and arithmetic. If he was going to be an officer in the army, he entered as a cadet in a military school which was attached to the royal stables. But if he was going to be a priest, he had to join one of the colleges which belonged to the different temples of the gods, and there, like Moses, he was instructed in all the wisdom of the Egyptians, and was taught all the strange ideas which they had about the gods, and the life after death, and the wonderful worlds, above and below, where the souls of men lived after they had finished their lives on earth.

But, whether his schooling was carried on to what we should call a University training or not, there was one thing that Tahuti was taught with the utmost care, and that was to be very respectful to those who were older than himself, never to sit down while an older person was standing in the room, and always to be very careful in his manners. Chief of the older people to whom he had to show respect were his parents, and above all, his mother, for the Egyptians reverenced their mothers more than anyone else in the world. Here is a little scrap of advice that a wise old Egyptian once left to his son: "Thou shalt never forget what thy mother has done for thee. She bare thee, and nourished thee in all manner of ways. She nursed thee for three years. She brought thee up, and when thou didst enter the school, and wast instructed in the writings, she came daily to thy master with bread and beer from her house. If thou forgettest her, she might blame thee; she might lift up her hands to God, and He would hear her complaint." Children nowadays might do a great deal worse than remember these wise words of the oldest book in the world.

But you are not to think that the Egyptian children's life was all teaching and prim behaviour. When Tahuti got his holidays, he would sometimes go out with his father and mother and sister on a fishing or fowling expedition. If they were going fishing, the little papyrus skiff was launched, and the party paddled away, armed with long thin spears, which had two prongs at the point. Drifting over the quiet shallow waters of the marshy lakes, they could see the fish swimming beneath them, and launch their spears at them. Sometimes, if he was lucky, Tahuti's father would pierce a fish with either prong of the spear, and then there was great excitement.

But still more interesting was the fowling among the marshes. The spears were laid aside on this kind of expedition, and instead, Tahuti and his father were armed with curved throw-sticks, shaped something like an Australian boomerang. But, besides the throw-sticks, they had with them a rather unusual helper. When people go shooting nowadays, they take dogs with them to retrieve the game. Well, the Egyptians had different kinds of dogs, too, which they used for hunting; but when they went fowling they took with them a cat which was trained to catch the wounded birds and bring them to her master. The little skiff was paddled cautiously across the marsh, and in among the reeds where the wild ducks and other waterfowl lived,

Sen-senb and her mother holding on to the tall
papyrus plants and pulling them aside to make room
for the boat, or plucking the beautiful lotus-lilies, of
which the Egyptians were so fond. When the birds
rose, Tahuti and his father let fly their throw-sticks,
and when a bird was knocked down, the cat, which
had been sitting quietly in the bow of the boat,
dashed forward among the reeds and secured the
fluttering creature before it could escape.

Altogether, it was great fun for the brother and
sister, as well as for the grown folks, and Tahuti and
Sen-senb liked nothing so well as when the gaily-
painted little skiff was launched for a day on the
marshes. I think that, on the whole, they had a very
bright and happy life in these old days, and that,
though they had not many of the advantages that
you have to-day, the boys and girls of three
thousand years ago managed to enjoy themselves in
their own simple way quite as well as you do now.

CHAPTER VII

SOME FAIRY-TALES OF LONG AGO

The little brown boys and girls who lived in Egypt
three thousand years ago were just as fond as you
are of hearing wonderful stories that begin with
"Once upon a time;" and I want in this chapter to
tell you some of the tales that Tahuti and Sen-senb
used to listen to in the evening when school was
over and play was done--the oldest of all wonder-

tales, stories that were old and had long been forgotten, ages before The Sleeping Beauty and Jack and the Beanstalk were first thought of.

One day, when King Khufu, the great King who built the biggest of the Pyramids, had nothing else to do, he called his sons and his wise men together, and said, "Is there anyone among you who can tell me the tales of the old magicians?" Then the King's son, Prince Baufra, stood up and said, "Your Majesty, I can tell you of a wonder that happened in the days of your father, King Seneferu. It fell on a day that the King grew weary of everything, and sought through all his palace for something to please him, but found nothing. Then he said to his officers, 'Bring to me the magician Zazamankh.' And when the magician came, the King said to him, 'O Zazamankh, I have sought through all my palace for some delight, and I have found none.' Then said Zazamankh, 'Let thy Majesty go in thy boat upon the lake of the palace, and let twenty beautiful girls be brought to row thee, and let their oars be of ebony, inlaid with gold and silver. And I myself will go with thee; and the sight of the water-birds, and the fair shores, and the green grass will cheer thy heart.' So the King and the wizard went down to the lake, and the twenty maidens rowed them about in the King's pleasure-galley. Nine rowed on this side, and nine on that, and the two fairest stood by the two rudders at the stern, and set the rowing song, each for her own side. And the King's heart grew glad and light, as the boat sped hither and thither, and the oars flashed in the sunshine to the song of the rowers.

"But as the boat turned, the top of the steering-oar struck the hair of one of the maidens who steered, and knocked her coronet of turquoise into the water; and she stopped her song, and all the rowers on her side stopped rowing. Then his Majesty said, 'Why have you stopped rowing, little one?' And the maiden answered, 'It is because my jewel of turquoise has fallen into the water.' 'Row on,' said the King, 'and I will give you another.' But the girl answered, 'I want my own one back, as I had it before.' So King Seneferu called Zazamankh to come to him, and said, 'Now, Zazamankh, I have done as you advised, and my heart is light; but, behold, the coronet of this little one has fallen into the water, and she has stopped singing, and spoiled the rowing of her side; and she will not have a new jewel, but wants the old one back again.'

"Then Zazamankh the wizard stood up in the King's boat, and spoke wonderful words. And, lo! the water of one half of the lake rose up, and heaped itself upon the top of the water of the other half, so that it was twice as deep as it was before. And the King's bark rode upon the top of the piled-up waters; but beyond it the bottom of the lake lay bare, with the shells and pebbles shining in the sunlight. And there, upon a broken shell, lay the little rower's coronet. Then Zazamankh leaped down and picked it up, and brought it to the King. And he spake wonderful words again, and the water sank down, and covered the whole bed of the lake, as it had done at first. So his Majesty spent a joyful day, and gave great rewards to the wizard Zazamankh."

When King Khufu heard that story, he praised the
men of olden times. But another of his sons, Prince
Hordadef, stood up, and said, "O King, that is only
a story of bygone days, and no one knows whether
it is true or a lie; but I will show thee a magician of
to-day." "Who is he, Hordadef?" said King Khufu.
And Hordadef answered, "His name is Dedi. He is a
hundred and ten years old, and every day he eats
five hundred loaves of bread, and a side of beef, and
drinks a hundred jugs of beer. He knows how to
fasten on a head that has been cut off. He knows
how to make a lion of the desert follow him, and he
knows the plan of the house of God that you have
wanted to know for so long."

Then King Khufu sent Prince Hordadef to bring
Dedi to him, and he brought Dedi back in the royal
boat. The King came out, and sat in the colonnade
of the palace, and Dedi was led before him. Then
said his Majesty, "Why have I never seen you
before, Dedi?" And Dedi answered, "Life, health,
strength to your Majesty! A man can only come
when he is called." "Is it true, Dedi, that you can
fasten on a head which has been cut off?"
"Certainly I can, your Majesty." Then said the King,
"Let a prisoner be brought from the prison, and let
his head be struck off." But Dedi said, "Long life to
your Majesty; do not try it on a man. Let us try a
bird or an animal."

So a goose was brought; its head was cut off; and
the head was laid at the east side of the hall, and the
body at the west. Then Dedi rose, and spoke
wonderful words. And, behold! the body of the
goose waddled to meet the head, and the head came

to meet the body. They joined together before his Majesty's throne, and the goose stood up and cackled.

Then, when Dedi had joined to its body again the head that had been struck off from an ox, and the ox followed him lowing, King Khufu said to him, "Is it true, O Dedi, that you know the plans of the house of God?" "It is true, your Majesty; but it is not I who shall give them to you." "Who, then?" said the King. "It is the eldest of three sons who shall be born to the lady Rud-didet, wife of the priest of Ra, the Sun-God. And Ra has promised that these three sons shall reign over this kingdom of thine." When King Khufu heard that word, his heart was troubled; but Dedi said, "Let not your Majesty's heart be troubled. Thy son shall reign first, then thy son's son, and then one of these." So the King commanded that Dedi should live in the house of Prince Hordadef; and that every day there should be given to him a thousand loaves, a hundred jugs of beer, an ox, and a hundred bunches of onions!

When the three sons of Rud-didet were born, Ra sent four goddesses to be their godmothers. They came attired like travelling dancing-girls; and one of the gods came with them, dressed like a porter. And when they had nursed the three children awhile, Rud-didet's husband said to them, "My ladies, what wages shall I give you?" So he gave them a bushel of barley, and they went away with their wages. But when they had gone a little way, Isis, the chief of them, said, "Why have we not done a wonder for these children?" So they stopped, and made crowns, the red crown and the white crown of

Egypt, and hid them in the bushel of barley, and sealed the sack, and put it in Rud-didet's store-chamber, and went away again.

A fortnight later, when Rud-didet was going to brew the household beer, there was no barley. And her maidservant said, "There is a bushel, but it was given to the dancing-girls, and lies in the store-room, sealed with their seal." So the lady said to her maid, "Go down and fetch it, and we shall give them more when they need it." The maid went down, but when she came to the store-room, lo! from within there came a sound of singing and dancing, and all such music as should be heard in a King's Court. So in fear she crept back to her mistress and told her, and Rud-didet went down and heard the royal music, and she told her husband when he came home at night, and their hearts were glad because their sons were to be Kings.

But after a time the lady Rud-didet quarrelled with her maid, and gave her a beating, as ladies sometimes did in those days; and the weeping maid said to her fellow-servants, "Shall she do this to me? She has borne three Kings, and I will go and tell it to his Majesty, King Khufu." So she stole away first to her uncle, and told him of her plot; but he was angry because she wished to betray the children to King Khufu, and he beat her with a scourge of flax. And as she went away by the side of the river a great crocodile came out of the water, and carried her off.... But here, alas! our story breaks off; the rest of the book is lost, and we cannot tell whether King Khufu tried to kill the three royal babies or not. Only we do know that the

first three Kings of the race which succeeded the
race of Khufu bore the same names as Rud-didet's
three babies, and were called, like all the Kings of
Egypt after them, "Sons of the Sun."

These, then, are absolutely the oldest fairy-stories in
the world, and if they do not seem very wonderful
to you, you must remember that everything has to
have a beginning, and that the people who made
these tales hadn't had very much practice in the art
of story-telling.

CHAPTER VIII

SOME FAIRY-TALES OF LONG AGO
(Continued)

Our next story belongs to a time several hundred
years later, and I dare say it seemed as wonderful to
the little Egyptians as the story of Sindbad the
Sailor does to you. It is called "The Story of the
Shipwrecked Sailor," and the sailor himself tells it
to a noble Egyptian.

"I was going," he says, "to the mines of Pharaoh,
and we set sail in a ship of 150 cubits long and 40
cubits wide (225 feet by 60 feet--quite a big ship for
the time). We had a crew of 150 of the best sailors
of Egypt, men whose hearts were as bold as lions.
They all foretold a happy voyage, but as we came
near the shore a great storm blew, the sea rose in
terrible waves, and our ship was fairly

overwhelmed. Clinging to a piece of wood, I was washed about for three days, and at last tossed up on an island; but not one was left of all my shipmates--all perished in the waves.

"I lay down in the shade of some bushes, and when I had recovered a little, I looked about me for food. There was plenty on every hand--figs and grapes, berries and corn, with all manner of birds. When my hunger was satisfied, I lit a fire, and made an offering to the gods who had saved me. Suddenly I heard a noise like thunder; the trees shook, and the earth quaked. Looking round, I saw a great serpent approaching me. He was nearly 50 feet long, and had a beard 3 feet in length. His body shone in the sun like gold, and when he reared himself up from his coils before me I fell upon my face.

"Then the serpent began to speak: 'What has brought thee, little one, what has brought thee? If thou dost not tell me quickly what has brought thee to this isle, I shall make thee vanish like a flame.' So saying, he took me up in his mouth, carried me gently to his lair, and laid me down unhurt; and again he said, 'What has brought thee, little one, what has brought thee to this isle of the sea?' So I told him the story of our shipwreck, and how I alone had escaped from the fury of the waves. Then said he to me: 'Fear not, little one, and let not thy face be sad. If thou hast come to me, it is God who has brought thee to this isle, which is filled with all good things. And now, see: thou shalt dwell for four months in this isle, and then a ship of thine own land shall come, and thou shalt go home to thy country, and die in thine own town. As for me, I am here with my brethren and my children. There are seventy-five of us in all, besides a young girl, who came here by chance, and was burned by fire from heaven. But if thou art strong and patient, thou shalt yet embrace thy children and thy wife, and return to thy home.'

"Then I bowed low before him, and promised to tell of him to Pharaoh, and to bring him ships full of all the treasures of Egypt; but he smiled at my speech, and said, 'Thou hast nothing that I need, for I am Prince of the Land of Punt, and all its perfumes are mine. Moreover, when thou departest, thou shalt never again see this isle, for it shall be changed into waves.'

"Now, behold! when the time was come, as he had foretold, the ship drew near. And the good serpent said to me, 'Farewell, farewell! go to thy home, little one, see again thy children, and let thy name be good in thy town; these are my wishes for thee.' So I bowed low before him, and he loaded me with precious gifts of perfume, cassia, sweet woods, ivory, baboons, and all kinds of precious things, and I embarked in the ship. And now, after a voyage of two months, we are coming to the house of Pharaoh, and I shall go in before Pharaoh, and offer the gifts which I have brought from this isle into Egypt, and Pharaoh shall thank me before the great ones of the land."

Our last story belongs to a later age than that of the Shipwrecked Sailor. About 1,500 years before Christ there arose in Egypt a race of mighty soldier-Kings, who founded a great empire, which stretched

from the Soudan right through Syria and
Mesopotamia as far as the great River Euphrates.
Mesopotamia, or Naharaina, as the Egyptians called
it, had been an unknown land to them before this
time; but now it became to them what America was
to the men of Queen Elizabeth's time, or the heart of
Africa to your grandfathers--the wonderful land of
romance, where all kinds of strange things might
happen. And this story of the Doomed Prince,
which I have to tell you, belongs partly to
Naharaina, and, as you will see, some of our own
fairy-stories have been made out of very much the
same materials as are used in it.

Once upon a time there was a King in Egypt who
had no child. His heart was grieved because he had
no child, and he prayed to the gods for a son; so in
course of time a son was born to him, and the Fates
(like fairy godmothers) came to his cradle to foretell
what should happen to him. And when they saw
him, they said, "His doom is to die either by the
crocodile, or by the serpent, or by the dog." When
the King heard this, his heart was sore for his little
son, and he resolved that he would put the boy
where no harm could come to him; so he built for
him a beautiful house away in the desert, and
furnished it with all kinds of fine things, and sent
the boy there, with faithful servants to guard him,
and to see that he came to no hurt. So the boy grew
up quietly and safely in his house in the desert.

But it fell on a day that the young Prince looked out
from the roof of his house, and he saw a man
walking across the desert, with a dog following
him. So he said to the servant who was with him,

"What is this that walks behind the man who is coming along the road?" "It is a dog," said the page. Then the boy said, "You must bring me one like him," and the page went and told His Majesty. Then the King said, "Get a little puppy, and take it to him, lest his heart be sad." So they brought him a little dog, and it grew up along with him.

Now, it happened that, when the boy had grown to be a strong young man, he grew weary of being always shut up in his fine house. Therefore he sent a message to his father, saying, "Why am I always to be shut up here? Since I am doomed to three evil Fates, let me have my desire, and let God do what is in His heart." So the King agreed, and they gave the young Prince arms, and sent him away to the eastern frontier, and his dog went with him, and they said to him, "Go wherever you will." So he went northward through the desert, he and his dog, until he came to the land of Naharaina.

Now, the chief of the land of Naharaina had no children, save one beautiful daughter, and for her he had built a wonderful house. It had seventy windows, and it stood on a great rock more than 100 feet high. And the chief summoned the sons of all the chiefs of the country round about, and said to them, "The Prince who can climb to my daughter's window shall have her for his wife." So all the young Princes of the land camped around the house, and tried every day to climb to the window of the beautiful Princess; but none of them succeeded, for the rock was very steep and high.

Then, one day when they were climbing as they

were wont, the young Prince of Egypt rode by with his dog; and the Princes welcomed him, bathed him, and fed his horse, and said to him, "Whence comest thou, thou goodly youth?" He did not wish to tell them that he was the son of Pharaoh, so he answered, "I am the son of an Egyptian officer. My father married a second wife, and, when she had children, she hated me, and drove me away from my home." So they took him into their company, and he stayed with them many days.

Now, it fell on a day that he asked them, "Why do you stay here, trying always to climb this rock?" And they told him of the beautiful Princess who lived in the house on the top of the rock, and how the man who could climb to her window should marry her. Therefore the young Prince of Egypt climbed along with them, and it came to pass that at last he climbed to the window of the Princess; and when she saw him, she fell in love with him, and kissed him.

Then was word sent to the Chief of Naharaina that one of the young men had climbed to his daughter's window, and he asked which of the Princes it was, and the messenger said, "It is not a Prince, but the son of an Egyptian officer, who has been driven away from Egypt by his stepmother." Then the Chief of Naharaina was very angry, and said, "Shall I give my daughter to an Egyptian fugitive? Let him go back to Egypt." But, when the messengers came to tell the young man to go away, the Princess seized his hand, and said, "If you take him from me, I will not eat; I will not drink; I shall die in that same hour." Then the chief sent men to kill the youth where he was in the house. But the Princess said, "If you kill him, I shall be dead before the sun goes down. I will not live an hour if I am parted from him." So the chief was obliged to agree to the marriage; and the young Prince was married to the Princess, and her father gave them a house, and slaves, and fields, and all sorts of good things.

But after a time the young Prince said to his wife, "I am doomed to die, either by a crocodile, or by a serpent, or by a dog." And his wife answered, "Why, then, do you keep this dog always with you? Let him be killed." "Nay," said he, "I am not going to kill my faithful dog, which I have brought up since the time that he was a puppy." So the Princess feared greatly for her husband, and would never let him go out of her sight.

Now, it happened in course of time that the Prince went back to the land of Egypt; and his wife went with him, and his dog, and he dwelt in Egypt. And one day, when the evening came, he grew drowsy, and fell asleep; and his wife filled a bowl with milk, and placed it by his side, and sat to watch him as he slept. Then a great serpent came out of his hole to bite the youth. But his wife was watching, and she made the servants give the milk to the serpent, and he drank till he could not move. Then the Princess killed the serpent with blows of her dagger. So she woke her husband, and he was astonished to see the serpent lying dead, and his faithful wife said to him, "Behold, God has given one of thy dooms into thy hand; He will also give the others." And the Prince made sacrifice to God, and praised Him.

Now, it fell on a day that the Prince went out to
walk in his estate, and his dog went with him. And
as they walked, the dog ran after some game, and
the Prince followed the dog. They came to the River
Nile, and the dog went into the river, and the Prince
followed him. Then a great crocodile rose in the
river, and laid hold on the youth, and said, "I am thy
doom, following after thee." ...

But just here the old papyrus roll on which the story
is written is torn away, and we do not know what
happened to the Doomed Prince. I fancy that, in
some way or other, his dog would save him from
the crocodile, and that later, by some accident, the
poor faithful dog would be the cause of his master's
death. At least, it looks as if the end of the story
must have been something like that; for the
Egyptians believed that no one could escape from
the doom that was laid upon him, but had to suffer
it sooner or later. Perhaps, some day, one of the
explorers who are searching the land of Egypt for
relics of the past may come on another papyrus roll
with the end of the story, and then we shall find out
whether the dog did kill the Prince, or whether God
gave all his dooms into his hand, as his wife hoped.

These are some of the stories that little Tahuti and
Sen-senb used to listen to in the long evenings
when they were tired of play. Perhaps they seem
very simple and clumsy to you; but I have no doubt
that, when they were told in those old days, the
black eyes of the little Egyptian boys and girls used
to grow very big and round, and the wizard who
could fasten on heads which had been cut off
seemed a very wonderful person, and the talking

serpents and crocodiles seemed very real and very dreadful.

Anyhow, you have heard the oldest stories in all the world--the fathers and mothers, so to speak, of all the great family of wonder-tales that have delighted and terrified children ever since.

CHAPTER IX

EXPLORING THE SOUDAN

There is no more wonderful or interesting story than that which tells how bit by bit the great dark continent of Africa has been explored, and made to yield up its secrets. But did you ever think what a long story it is, and how very early it begins? It is in Egypt that we find the first chapters of the story; and they can still be read, written in the quaint old picture writing which the Egyptians used, on the rock tombs of a place in the south of Egypt, called Elephantine.

In early days the land of Egypt used to end at what was called the First Cataract of the Nile, a place where the river came down in a series of rapids among a lot of rocky islets. The First Cataract has disappeared now, for British engineers have made a great dam across the Nile just at this point, and turned the whole country, for miles above the dam, into a lake. But in those days the Egyptians used to believe that the Nile, to which they owed so much, began at the First Cataract. Yet they knew of the wild country of Nubia beyond and, in very early times indeed, about 5,000 years ago, they used to send exploring expeditions into that half-desert land which we have come to know as the Soudan.

Near the First Cataract there lies the island of Elephantine, and when the Egyptian kingdom was young the great barons who owned this island were the Lords of the Egyptian Marches, just as the Percies and the Douglases were the Lords of the Marches in England and Scotland. It was their duty to keep in order the wild Nubian tribes south of the Cataract, to see that they allowed the trading caravans to pass safely, and sometimes to lead these caravans through the desert themselves. A caravan was a very different thing then from the long train of camels that we think of now when we hear the name. For, though there are some very old pictures which show that, before Egyptian history begins at all, the camel was known in Egypt, somehow that useful animal seems to have disappeared from the land for many hundreds of years. The Pharaohs and their adventurous barons never used the queer, ungainly creature that carries the desert postman in our picture, and the ivory, gold-dust, and ebony that came from the Soudan had to be carried on the backs of hundreds of asses.

The barons of Elephantine bore the proud title of "Keepers of the Door of the South," and, in addition, they display, seemingly just as proudly, the title "Caravan Conductors." In those days it was no easy task to lead a caravan through the Soudan, and bring it back safe with its precious load through all the wild and savage tribes who inhabited the land of Nubia. More than one of the barons of Elephantine set out with a caravan never to return, but to leave his bones, and those of his companions, to whiten among the desert sands; and one of them has told us how, hearing that his father had been killed on one of these adventurous journeys, he mustered his retainers, marched south with a train of a hundred asses, punished the tribe which had been guilty of the deed, and brought his father's body home, to be buried with all due honours.

Some of the records of these early journeys, the first attempts to explore the interior of Africa, may still be read, carved on the walls of the tombs where the brave explorers sleep. One baron, called Herkhuf, has told us of no fewer than four separate expeditions which he made into the Soudan. On his first journey, as he was still young, he went in company with his father, and was away for seven months. The next time he was allowed to go alone, and brought back his caravan safely after an absence of eight months.

On his third journey he went farther than before, and gathered so large a quantity of ivory and gold-dust that three hundred asses were required to bring his treasure home. So rich a caravan was a tempting prize for the wild tribes on the way; but Herkhuf persuaded one of the Soudanese chiefs to furnish him with a large escort, and the caravan was so strongly guarded that the other tribes did not venture to attack it, but were glad to help its leader with guides and gifts of cattle. Herkhuf brought his treasures safely back to Egypt, and the King was so pleased with his success that he sent a special messenger with a boat full of delicacies to refresh the weary traveller.

But the most successful of all his expeditions was the fourth. The King who had sent him on the other journeys had died, and was succeeded by a little boy called Pepy, who was only about six years old when he came to the throne, and who reigned for more than ninety years--the longest reign in the world's history. In the second year of Pepy's reign, the bold Herkhuf set out again for the Soudan, and this time, along with other treasures, he brought back something that his boy-King valued far more than gold or ivory.

You know how, when Stanley went in search of Emin Pasha, he discovered in the Central African forests a strange race of dwarfs, living by themselves, and very shy of strangers. Well, for all these thousands of years, the forefathers of these little dwarfs must have been living in the heart of the Dark Continent. In early days they evidently lived not so far away from Egypt as when Stanley found them, for, on at least one occasion, one of Pharaoh's servants had been able to capture one of the little men, and bring him down as a present to his master, greatly to the delight of the King and Court. Herkhuf was equally fortunate. He managed to secure a dwarf from one of these pigmy tribes, and brought him back with his caravan, that he might please the young King with his quaint antics and his curious dances.

When the King heard of the present which his brave

servant was bringing back for him, he was wild
with delight. The thought of this new toy was far
more to the little eight-year-old, King though he
was, than all the rest of the treasure which Herkhuf
had gathered; and he caused a letter to be written to
the explorer, telling him of his delight, and giving
him all kinds of advice as to how careful he should
be that the dwarf should come to no harm on the
way to Court.

The letter, through all its curious old phrases, is
very much the kind of letter that any boy might send
on hearing of some new toy that was coming to him.
"My Majesty," says the little eight-year-old
Pharaoh, "wisheth to see this pigmy more than all
the tribute of Punt. And if thou comest to Court
having this pigmy with thee sound and whole, My
Majesty will do for thee more than King Assa did
for the Chancellor Baurded." (This was the man
who had brought back the other dwarf in earlier
days.) Little King Pepy then gives careful directions
that Herkhuf is to provide proper people to see that
the precious dwarf does not fall into the Nile on his
way down the river; and these guards are to watch
behind the place where he sleeps, and look into his
bed ten times each night, that they may be sure that
nothing has gone wrong.

The poor little dwarf must have had rather an
uncomfortable time of it, one fancies, if his sleep
was to be broken so often. Perhaps there was more
danger of killing him with kindness and care, than if
they had left him more to himself; but Pepy's
anxiety was very like a boy. However, Herkhuf
evidently succeeded in bringing his dwarf safe and

sound to the King's Court, and no doubt the quaint
little savage proved a splendid toy for the young
King. One wonders what he thought of the great
cities and the magnificent Court of Egypt, and
whether his heart did not weary sometimes for the
wild freedom of his lost home.

Herkhuf was so proud of the King's letter that he
caused it to be engraved, word for word, on the
walls of the tomb which he hewed out for himself at
Elephantine, and there to this day the words can be
read which tell us how old is the story of African
exploration, and how a boy was always just a boy,
even though he lived five thousand years ago, and
reigned over a great kingdom.

CHAPTER X

A VOYAGE OF DISCOVERY

About 3,500 years ago, there reigned a great Queen
in Egypt. It was not usual for the Egyptian throne to
be occupied by a woman, though great respect was
always shown to women in Egypt, and the rank of a
King's mother was considered quite as important as
that of his father. But once at least in her history
Egypt had a great Queen, whose fame deserves to
be remembered, and who takes honourable rank
among the great women, like Queen Elizabeth and
Queen Victoria, who have ruled kingdoms.

During part of her life Queen Hatshepsut was only

joint sovereign along with her husband, and in the latter part of her reign she was joint sovereign with her half-brother or nephew, who succeeded her; but for at least twenty years she was really the sole ruler of Egypt, and governed the land wisely and well.

Perhaps the most interesting thing that happened in her reign was the voyage of discovery which she caused to be made by some ships of her fleet. Centuries before her time, when the world was young, the Egyptians had made expeditions down the Red Sea to a land which they sometimes called Punt, and sometimes "The Divine Land." Probably it was part of the country that we now know as Somaliland. But for a very long time these voyages had ceased, and people only knew by hearsay, and by the stories of ancient days, of this wonderful country that lay away by the Southern Sea.

One day, the Queen tells us, she was at prayers in the temple of the god Amen at Thebes, when she felt a sudden inspiration. The god was giving her a command to send an expedition to this almost forgotten land. "A command was heard in the sanctuary, a behest of the god himself, that the ways which lead to Punt should be explored, and that the roads to the Ladders of Incense should be trodden." In obedience to this command, the Queen at once equipped a little fleet of the quaint old galleys that the Egyptians then used, and sent them out, with picked crews, and a royal envoy in command, to sail down the Red Sea, in search of the Divine Land. The ships were laden with all kinds of goods to barter with the Punites, and a guard of Egyptian soldiers was placed on board.

We do not know how long it took the little squadron to reach its destination. Sea voyages in those days were slow and dangerous. But at last the ships safely reached the mouth of the Elephant River in Somaliland, and went up the river with the tide till they came to the village of the natives. They found that the Punites lived in curious beehive-shaped houses, some of them made of wicker-work, and placed on piles, so that they had to climb into them by ladders. The men were not negroes, though some negroes lived among them; they were very much like the Egyptians in appearance, wore pointed beards, and were dressed only in loincloths, while the women wore a yellow sleeveless dress, which reached halfway between the knee and ankle.

Nehsi, the royal envoy, landed with an officer and eight soldiers, and, to show that he came in peace, he spread out on a table some presents for the chief of the Punites--five bracelets, two gold necklaces, a dagger, with belt and sheath, a battle-axe, and eleven strings of glass beads--much such a present as a European explorer might give to-day to an African chief. The natives came down in great excitement to see the strangers who had brought such treasures, and were astonished at the arrival of such a fleet. "How is it," they said, "that you have reached this country, hitherto unknown to men? Have you come by way of the sky, or have you sailed on the waters of the Divine Sea?" The chief, who was called Parihu, came down with his wife Aty, and his daughter. Aty rode down on a donkey, but dismounted to see the strangers, and, indeed, the poor donkey must have been greatly relieved, for the chieftainess was an exceedingly fat lady, and her daughter, though so young, showed every intention of being as fat as her mother.

After the envoy and the chief had exchanged compliments, business began. The Egyptians pitched a tent in which they stored their goods for barter, and to put temptation out of the way of the natives, they drew a guard of soldiers round the tent. For several days the market remained open, and the country people brought down their treasures, till the ships were laden as deeply as was safe. The cargo was a varied and valuable one. Elephants' tusks, gold, ebony, apes, greyhounds, leopard skins, all were crowded into the galleys, the apes sitting gravely on the top of the bales of goods, and looking longingly at the land which they were leaving.

But the most important part of the cargo was the incense, and the incense-trees. Great quantities of the gum from which the incense was made were placed on board, and also thirty-one of the incense sycamores, their roots carefully surrounded with a large ball of earth, and protected by baskets. Several young chiefs of the Punites accompanied the expedition back to Thebes, to see what life was like in the strange new world which had been revealed to them. Altogether the voyage home must have been no easy undertaking, for the ships, with their heavy cargoes, must have been very difficult to handle.

The arrival of the squadron at Thebes, which they must have reached by a canal connecting the Nile with the Red Sea, was made the occasion of a great holiday festival. Long lines of troops in gala attire came out to meet the brave explorers, and an escort of the royal fleet accompanied the exploring squadron up to the temple quay where the ships were to moor. Then the Thebans feasted their eyes on the wonderful treasures that had come from Punt, wondering at the natives, the incense, the ivory, and, above all, at a giraffe which had been brought home. How the poor creature was stowed away on the little Egyptian ship it is hard to see; but there he was, with his spots and his long neck, the most wonderful creature that the good folks of Thebes had ever seen. The precious incense gum was stored in the temple, and the Queen herself gave a bushel measure, made of a mixture of gold and silver, to measure it out with.

So the voyage of discovery had ended in a great success. But Queen Hatshepsut's purpose was only half fulfilled as yet. In a nook of the limestone cliffs, not far from Thebes, her father before her had begun to build a very wonderful temple, close beside the ruins of an older sanctuary which had stood there for hundreds of years. Hatshepsut had been gradually completing his work, and the temple was now growing into a most beautiful building, very different from ordinary Egyptian temples. From the desert sands in front it rose terrace above terrace, each platform bordered with rows of beautiful limestone pillars, until at last it reached the cliffs, and the most sacred chamber of it, the Holy of Holies, was hewn into the solid wall of rock behind.

This temple the Queen resolved to make into what

she called a Paradise for Amen, the god who had told her to send out the ships. So she planted on the terraces the sacred incense-trees which had been brought from Punt; and, thanks to careful tending and watering, they flourished well in their new home. And then, all along the walls of the temple, she caused her artists to carve and paint the whole story of the voyage. We do not know the names of the artists who did the work, though we know that of the architect, Sen-mut, who planned the building. But, whoever they were, they must have been very skilful sculptors; for the story of the voyage is told in pictures on the walls of this wonderful temple, so that everything can be seen just as it actually happened more than three thousand years ago.

You can see the ships toiling along with oar and sail towards their destination, the meeting with the natives, the palaver and the trading, the loading of the galleys, and the long procession of Theban soldiers going out to meet the returning explorers. Not a single detail is missed, and, thanks to the Queen and her artists, we can go back over all these years, and see how sailors worked, and how people lived in savage lands in that far-off time, and realize that explorers dealt with the natives in foreign countries in those days very much as they deal with them now. When our explorers of to-day come back from their journeys, they generally tell the story of their adventures in a big book with many pictures; but no explorer ever published the account of a voyage of discovery on such a scale as did Queen Hatshepsut, when she carved the voyage to Punt on the walls of her great temple at Deir-el-Bahri, and no pictures in any modern book are likely to last as

long, or to tell so much as these pictures that have
come to light again during the last few years, after
being buried for centuries under the desert sands.

Queen Hatshepsut has left other memorials of her
greatness besides the temple with its story of her
voyage. She has told us how one day she was sitting
in her palace, and thinking of her Creator, when the
thought came into her mind to rear two great
obelisks before the Temple of Amen at Karnak. So
she gave the command, and Sen-mut, her clever
architect, went up the Nile to Aswan, and quarried
two huge granite blocks, and floated them down the
river. Cleopatra's Needle, which stands on the
Thames Embankment, is 68-1/2 feet high, and it
seems to us a huge stone for men to handle. Our
own engineers had trouble enough in bringing it to
this country, and setting it up. But these two great
obelisks of Queen Hatshepsut were 98-1/2 feet
high, and weighed about 350 tons apiece. Yet Sen-
mut had them quarried, and set up, and carved all
over from base to summit in seven months from the
time when the Queen gave her command! One of
them still stands at Karnak, the tallest obelisk in the
temple there; while the other great shaft has fallen,
and lies broken, close to its companion. They tell us
their own plain story of the wisdom and skill of
those far-off days; and perhaps the great Queen who
thought of her Creator as she sat in her palace, and
longed to honour Him, found that the God whom
she ignorantly worshipped was indeed not far from
His servant's heart.

CHAPTER XI

EGYPTIAN BOOKS

The Egyptians were, if not quite the earliest, at least among the earliest of all the peoples of the world to find out how to put down their thoughts in writing, or in other words, to make a book; and one of their old books, full of wise advice from a father to his son, is, perhaps, the oldest book in the world. Two words which we are constantly using might help to remind us of how much we owe to their cleverness. The one is "Bible," and the other is "paper." When we talk of the Bible, which just means "the Book," we are using one of the words which the Greeks used to describe the plant out of which the Egyptians made the material on which they wrote; and when we talk of paper, we are using another name, the commoner name, of the same plant. For the Egyptians were the first people to make paper, and they used it for many centuries before other people had learned how much handier it was than the other things which they used.

Yet, if you saw an Egyptian book, you would think it was a very curious and clumsy thing indeed, and very different from the handy volumes which we use nowadays. When an Egyptian wanted to make a book, he gathered the stems of a kind of reed called the papyrus, which grew in some parts of Egypt in marshy ground. This plant grew to a height of from 12 to 15 feet, and had a stalk about 6 inches thick. The outer rind was peeled off this stalk, and then the inner part of it was separated, by means of a flat needle, into thin layers. These layers were joined to one another on a table, and a thin gum was spread over them, and then another layer was laid crosswise on the top of the first. The double sheet thus made was then put into a press, squeezed together, and dried. The sheets varied, of course, in breadth according to the purpose for which they were needed. The broadest that we know of measure about 17 inches across, but most are much narrower than that.

When the Egyptian had got his paper, he did not make it up into a volume with the sheets bound together at the back, as we do. He joined them end to end, adding on sheet after sheet as he wrote, and rolling up his book as he went along; so when the book was done it formed a big roll, sometimes many feet long. There is one great book in the British Museum which measures 135 feet in length. You would think it very strange and awkward to have to handle a book like that.

But if the book seemed curious to you, the writing in it would seem still more curious; for the Egyptian writing was certainly the quaintest, and perhaps the prettiest, that has ever been known. It is called "hieroglyphic," which means "sacred carving," and it is nothing but little pictures from beginning to end. The Egyptians began by putting down a picture of the thing which was represented by the word they wanted to use, and, though by-and-by they formed a sort of alphabet to spell words with, and had, besides, signs that represented the different syllables of a word, still, these signs were all little pictures. For instance, one of their signs for a was the figure of an eagle; their sign for m was a lion,

and for u a little chicken; so that when you look at
an Egyptian book written in the hieroglyphic
character, you see column after column of birds and
beasts and creeping things, of men and women and
boats, and all sorts of other things, marching across
the page.

When the Egyptians wanted any of their writings to
last for a very long time, they did not trust them to
the frail papyrus rolls, but used another kind of
book altogether. You have heard of "sermons in
stones"? Well, a great many of the Egyptian books
that tell us of the great deeds of the Pharaohs were
written on stone, carved deep and clear in the hard
granite of a great obelisk, or in the limestone of a
temple wall. When one of the Kings came back
from the wars, he generally published the account
of his battles and victories by carving them on the
walls of one of the great temples, or on a pillar set
up in the court of a temple, and there they remain to
this day for scholars to read.

When the hieroglyphics were cut in stone, the lines
were often filled in with pastes of different colours,
so that the whole writing was a blaze of beautiful
tints, and the walls looked as if they were covered
with finely-coloured hangings. Of course, the
colours have mostly faded now; but there are still
some temples and tombs where they can be seen,
almost as fresh as when they were first laid on, and
from these we can gather some idea of how
wonderfully beautiful were these stone books of
ancient Egypt. The scribes and carvers knew very
well how beautiful their work was, and were careful
to make it look as beautiful as possible; so much so,

that if they found that the grouping of figures to make up a particular word or sentence was going to be ugly or clumsy, they would even prefer to spell the word wrong, rather than spoil the appearance of their picture-writing. Some of you, I dare say, spell words wrong now and again; but I fancy it isn't because you think they look prettier that way.

But now let us turn back again to our papyrus roll. Suppose that we have got it, clean and fresh, and that our friend the scribe is going to write upon it. How does he go about it? To begin with, he draws from his belt a long, narrow wooden case, and lays it down beside him. This is his palette; rather a different kind of palette from the one which artists use. It is a piece of wood, with one long hollow in it, and two or three shallow round ones. The long hollow holds a few pens, which are made out of thin reeds, bruised at the ends, so that their points are almost like little brushes. The shallow round hollows are for holding ink--black for most of the writing, red for special words, and perhaps one or two other colours, if the scribe is going to do a very fine piece of work. So he squats down, cross-legged, dips a reed-pen in the ink, and begins. As he writes he makes his little figures of men and beasts and birds face all in the one direction, and his readers will know that they must always read from the point towards which the characters face. Now and then, when he comes to some specially important part, he draws, in gay colours, a little picture of the scene which the words describe.

Now, you can understand that this picture-writing was not very easy work to do when you had nothing but a bruised reed to draw all sorts of animals with. Gradually the pictures grew less and less like the creatures they stood for to begin with, and at last the old hieroglyphic broke down into a kind of running hand, where a stroke or two might stand for an eagle, a lion, or a man. And very many of the Egyptian books are written in this kind of broken-down hieroglyphic, which is called "hieratic," or priestly writing. But some of the finest and costliest books were still written in the beautiful old style.

On their papyrus rolls the Egyptians wrote all sorts of things--books of wise advice, stories like the fairy-tales which we have been hearing, legends of the gods, histories, and poems; but the book that is oftenest met with is one of their religious books. It is nearly always called the "Book of the Dead" now, and some people call it the Egyptian Bible, but neither of these names is the right one. Certainly, it is not in the least like the Bible, and the Egyptians themselves never called it the Book of the Dead. They called it "The Chapters of Coming Forth by Day," and the reason they gave it that name was because they believed that if their dead friends knew all the wisdom that was written in it, they would escape all the dangers of the other world, and would be able in heaven to go in and out just as they had done upon earth, and to be happy for ever.

The book is full of all kinds of magical charms against the serpents and dragons and all the other kinds of evil things that sought to destroy the dead person in the other world. The scribes used to write off copies of it by the dozen, and keep them in stock, with blank places for the names of the persons who were to use them. When anyone died, his friends went away to a scribe, and bought a roll of the Book of the Dead, and the scribe filled in the name of the dead person in the blank places. Then the book was buried along with his mummy, so that when he met the demons and serpents on the road to heaven, he would know how to drive them away, and when he came to gates that had to be opened, or rivers that had to be crossed, he would know the right magical words to use.

Some of these rolls of the Book of the Dead are very beautifully written, and illustrated with most wonderful little coloured pictures, representing different scenes of life in the other world, and it is from these that we have learned a great deal of what the Egyptians believed about the judgment after death, and heaven. But the common ones are very carelessly done. The scribes knew that the book was going to be buried at once, and that nobody was likely ever to see it again; so they did not care much whether they made mistakes or not, and often they missed out parts of the book altogether. They little thought that, thousands of years after they were dead, scholars would dig up their writings again, and read them, and see all their blunders.

Of course, a great deal of this book is dreadful rubbish, and anything more unlike the noble and beautiful teaching of the Bible you can scarcely imagine. It has no more sense in it than the "Fee! fi! foh! fum!" of our fairy-stories. Here is one little chapter from it. It is called "The Chapter of Repulsing Serpents," and the Egyptians supposed that when a serpent attacked you on your way to heaven, you had only to recite this verse, and the serpent would be powerless to harm you: "Hail, thou serpent Rerek! advance not hither. Stand still now, and thou shalt eat the rat which is an abomination unto Ra (the Sun-God), and thou shalt crunch the bones of a filthy cat."

It sounds very silly, doesn't it? And there are many things quite as silly as this in the book. You can scarcely imagine how wise people like the Egyptians could ever have believed in such drivel. But, then, side by side with this miserable stuff, you find really wonderful and noble thoughts, that surely came to these men of ancient days from God Himself, telling them how every man must be judged at last for all that he has done on earth, and how only those who have done justly, and loved mercy, and walked humbly with God, will be accepted by Him.

CHAPTER XII

TEMPLES AND TOMBS

Anyone travelling through our own land, or through any European country, to see the great buildings of long ago, would find that they were nearly all either churches or castles. There are the great cathedrals, very beautiful and wonderful; and there are the great buildings, sometimes partly palaces and partly fortresses, where Kings and nobles lived in bygone days. Well, if you were travelling in Egypt to see its great buildings, you would find a difference. There are plenty of churches, or temples, rather, and very wonderful they are; but there are no castles or palaces left, or, at least, there are next to none. Instead of palaces and castles, you would find tombs. Egypt, in fact, is a land of great temples and great tombs.

Now, one can see why the Egyptians built great temples; for they were a very religious nation, and paid great honour to their gods. But why did they give so much attention to their tombs? The reason is, as you will hear more fully in another chapter, that there never was a nation which believed so firmly as did the Egyptians that the life after death was far more important than life in this world. They built their houses, and even their palaces, very lightly, partly of wood and partly of clay, because they knew that they were only to live in them for a few years. But they called their tombs "eternal dwelling-places"; and they have made them so wonderfully that they have lasted long after all the other buildings of the land, except the temples, have passed away.

First of all, let me try to give you an idea of what an Egyptian temple must have been like in the days of its splendour. People come from all parts of the world to see even the ruins of these buildings, and they are altogether the most astonishing buildings in the world; but they are now only the skeletons of what the temples once were, and scarcely give you any more idea of their former glory and beauty than a human skeleton does of the beauty of a living man or woman. Suppose, then, that we are coming up to

the gates of a great Egyptian temple in the days
when it was still the house of a god who was
worshipped by hundreds of thousands of people.

As we pass out of the narrow streets of the city to
which the temple belongs, we find ourselves
standing upon a broad paved way, which stretches
before us for hundreds of yards. On either side, this
way is bordered by a row of statues, and these
statues are in the form of what we call sphinxes--
that is to say, they have bodies shaped like
crouching lions, and on the lion-body there is set
the head of a different creature. Some of the
sphinxes, like the Great Sphinx, have human heads;
but those which border the temple avenues have
oftener either ram or jackal heads.

As we pass along the avenue, two high towers rise
before us, and between them is a great gateway. In
front of the gate-towers are two tall obelisks,
slender, tapering shafts of red granite, like
Cleopatra's Needle on the Thames Embankment.
They are hewn out of single blocks of stone, carved
all over with hieroglyphic figures, polished till they
shine like mirrors, and their pointed tops are gilded
so that they flash brilliantly in the sunlight. Beside
the obelisks, which may be from 70 to 100 feet
high, there are huge statues, perhaps two, perhaps
four, of the King who built the temple. These
statues represent the King as sitting upon his throne,
with the double crown of Egypt, red and white,
upon his head. They also are hewn out of single
blocks of stone, and when you look at the huge
figures you wonder how human hands could ever
get such stones out of the quarry, sculpture them,

and set them up. Before one of the temples of
Thebes still lie the broken fragments of a statue of
Ramses II. When it was whole the statue must have
been about 57 feet high, and the great block of
granite must have weighed about 1,000 tons--the
largest single stone that was ever handled by human
beings.

Fastened to the towers are four tall flagstaves--two
on either side of the gate--and from them float
gaily-coloured pennons. The walls of the towers are
covered with pictures of the wars of the King. Here
you see him charging in his chariot upon his fleeing
enemies; here, again, he is seizing a group of
captives by the hair, and raising his mace or his
sword to kill them; but whatever he is doing, he is
always gigantic, while his foes are mere helpless
human beings. All these carvings are brilliantly
painted, and the whole front of the building glows
with colour; it is really a kind of pictorial history of
the King's reign.

Now we stand in front of the gate. Its two leaves are
made of cedar-wood brought from Lebanon; but
you cannot see the wood at all, for it is overlaid
with plates of silver chased with beautiful designs.
Passing through the gateway, we find ourselves in a
broad open court. All round it runs a kind of
cloister, whose roof is supported upon tall pillars,
their capitals carved to represent the curving leaves
of the palm-tree. In the middle of the court there
stands a tall pillar of stone, inscribed with the story
of the great deeds of Pharaoh, and his gifts to the
god of the temple. It is inlaid with turquoise,
malachite, and lapis-lazuli, and sparkles with

precious stones.

At the farther side of this court, another pair of
towers and another gateway lead you into the
second court. Here we pass at once out of brilliant
sunlight into semi-darkness; for this court is entirely
roofed over, and no light enters it except from the
doorway and from grated slits in the roof. Look
around you, and you will see the biggest single
chamber that was ever built by the hands of man.
Down the centre run two lines of gigantic pillars
which hold up the roof, and form the nave of the
hall; and beyond these on either side are the aisles,
whose roofs are supported by a perfect forest of
smaller columns.

Look up to the twelve great pillars of the nave.
They soar above your head, seventy feet into the air,
their capitals bending outwards in the shape of open
flowers. On each capital a hundred men could stand
safely; and the great stone roofing beams that
stretch from pillar to pillar weigh a hundred tons
apiece. How were they ever brought to the place?
And, still more, how were they ever swung up to
that dizzy height, and laid in their places? Each of
the great columns is sculptured with figures and
gaily painted, and the surrounding walls of the hall
are all decorated in the same way. But when you
look at the pictures, you find that it is no longer the
wars of the King that are represented. The inside of
the temple is too holy for such things. Instead, you
have pictures of the gods, and of the King making
all kinds of offerings to them; and these pictures are
repeated again and again, with endless inscriptions,
telling of the great gifts which Pharaoh has given to

the temple.

Finally we pass into the Holy of Holies. Here no light of day ever enters at all. The chamber, smaller and lower than either of the others, is in darkness except for the dim light of the lamp carried by the attendant priest. Here stands the shrine, a great block of granite, hewn into a dwelling-place for the figure of the god. It is closed with cedar doors covered with gold plates, and the doors are sealed; but if we could persuade the priest to let us look within, we should see a small wooden figure something like the one that we saw carried through the streets of Thebes, dressed and painted, and surrounded by offerings of meat, drink, and flowers. For this little figure all the glories that we have passed through have been created: an army of priests attends upon it day by day, dresses and paints it, spreads food before it, offers sacrifices and sings hymns in its praise.

Behind the sanctuary lie storehouses, which hold corn and fruits and wines enough to supply a city in time of siege. The god is a great proprietor, holding more land than any of the nobles of the country. He has a revenue almost as great as that of Pharaoh himself. He has troops of his own, an army which obeys no orders but his. On the Red Sea he has one fleet, bringing to his temple the spices and incense of the Southland; and from the Nile mouths another fleet sails to bring home cedar-wood from Lebanon, and costly stuffs from Tyre. His priests have far more power than the greatest barons of the land, and Pharaoh, mighty as he is, would think twice before offending a band of men whose hatred could shake him on his throne. Such was an Egyptian temple 3,000 years ago, when Egypt was the greatest power in the world.

But if the temples of ancient Egypt are wonderful, the tombs are almost more wonderful still. Very early in their history the Egyptians began to show their sense of the importance of the life after death by raising huge buildings to hold the bodies of their great men. Even the earliest Kings, who lived before there was any history at all, had great underground chambers scooped out and furnished with all sorts of things for their use in the after-life. But it is when we come to that King Khufu, who figures in the fairy-stories of Zazamankh and Dedi, that we begin to understand what a wonderful thing an Egyptian tomb might be.

Not very far from Cairo, the modern capital of Egypt, a line of strange, pointed buildings rises against the sky on the edge of the desert. These are the Pyramids, the tombs of the great Kings of Egypt in early days, and if we want to know what Egyptian builders could do 4,000 years before Christ, we must look at them. Take the largest of them, the Great Pyramid, called the Pyramid of Cheops. Cheops is really Khufu, the King who was so much put out by Dedi's prophecy about Rud-didet's three babies. No such building was ever reared either before or since. It stands, even now, 450 feet in height, and before the peak was destroyed, it was about 30 feet higher. Each of its four sides measures over 750 feet in length, and it covers more than twelve acres of ground, the size of a pretty large field. But you will get the best idea of how tremendous a building it is when I tell you that if you used it as a quarry, you could build a town, big enough to hold all the people of Aberdeen, out of the Great Pyramid; or if you broke up the stones of which it is built, and laid them in a line a foot broad and a foot deep, the line would reach a good deal more than halfway round the world at the Equator. You would have some trouble in breaking up the stones, however; for many of the great blocks weigh from 40 to 50 tons apiece, and they are so beautifully fitted to one another that you could not get the edge of a sheet of paper into the joints!

Inside this great mountain of stone there are long passages leading to two small rooms in the centre of the Pyramid; and in one of these rooms, called "the King's Chamber," the body of the greatest builder the world has ever seen was laid in its stone coffin. Then the passages were closed with heavy plug-blocks of stone, so that no one should ever disturb the sleep of King Khufu. But, in spite of all precautions, robbers mined their way into the Pyramid ages ago, plundered the coffin, and scattered to the winds the remains of the King, so that, as Byron says, "Not a pinch of dust remains of Cheops."

The other pyramids are smaller, though, if the Great Pyramid had not been built, the Second and Third would have been counted world's wonders. Near the Second Pyramid sits the Great Sphinx. It is a huge statue, human-headed and lion-bodied, carved out of limestone rock. Who carved it, or whose face it bears, we do not certainly know; but there the great figure crouches, as it has crouched for countless ages, keeping watch and ward over the empty tombs where the Pharaohs of Egypt once slept, its head towering seventy feet into the air, its vast limbs and body stretching for two hundred feet along the sand, the strangest and most wonderful monument ever hewn by the hands of man.

Later on in Egyptian history the Kings and great folk grew tired of building pyramids, and the fashion changed. Instead of raising huge structures above ground, they began to hew out caverns in the rocks in which to lay their dead. Round about Thebes, the rocks on the western side of the Nile are honeycombed with these strange houses of the departed. Their walls, in many cases, are decorated with bright and cheerful pictures, showing scenes of the life which the dead man lived on earth. There he stands, or sits, placid and happy, with his wife beside him, while all around him his servants go about their usual work. They plough and hoe, sow and reap; they gather the grapes from the vines and put them into the winepress; or they bring the first-fruits of the earth to present them before their master. In other pictures you see the great man going out to his amusements, fishing, hunting, or fowling; or you are taken into the town, and see the tradesmen working, and the merchants, and townsfolk buying and selling in the bazaars. In fact, the whole of life in Ancient Egypt passes before your eyes as you go from chamber to chamber, and it is from these old tomb-pictures that we have learned the most of what we know of how people lived and worked in those long-past days.

In one wild rocky glen, called the "Valley of the

Kings," nearly all the later Pharaohs were buried, and to-day their tombs are one of the sights of Thebes. Let us look at the finest of them--the tomb of Sety I., the father of that Ramses II. of whom we have heard so much. Entering the dark doorway in the cliff, you descend through passage after passage and hall after hall, until at last you reach the fourteenth chamber, "the gold house of Osiris," 470 feet from the entrance, where the great King was laid in his magnificent alabaster coffin. The walls and pillars of each chamber are wonderfully carved and painted. The pillars show pictures of the King making offerings to the gods, or being welcomed by them, but the pictures on the walls are very strange and weird. They represent the voyage of the sun through the realms of the under-world, and all the dangers and difficulties which the soul of the dead man has to encounter as he accompanies the sun-bark on its journey. Serpents, bats, and crocodiles, spitting fire, or armed with spears, pursue the wicked. The unfortunates who fall into their power are tortured in all kinds of horrible ways; their hearts are torn out; their heads are cut off; they are boiled in caldrons, or hung head downwards over lakes of fire. Gradually the soul passes through all these dangers into the brighter scenes of the Fields of the Blessed, where the justified sow and reap and are happy. Finally, the King arrives, purified, at the end of his long journey, and is welcomed by the gods into the Abode of the Blessed, where he, too, dwells as a god in everlasting life.

The beautiful alabaster coffin in which the mummy of King Sety was laid is now in the Soane Museum, London. When it was discovered, nearly a century ago, it was empty, and it was not till 1872 that some modern tomb-robbers found the body of the King, along with other royal mummies, hidden away in a deep pit among the cliffs. Now it lies in the museum at Cairo, and you can see the face of this great King, its fine, proud features not so very much changed, we can well believe, from what they were when he reigned 3,200 years ago. In the same museum you can look upon the faces of Tahutmes III., the greatest soldier of Egypt; of Ramses II., the oppressor of the Israelites; and, perhaps most interesting of all, of Merenptah, the Pharaoh who hardened his heart when Moses pled with him to let the Hebrews go, and whose picked troops were drowned in the Red Sea as they pursued their escaping slaves.

It is very strange to think that one can see the actual features and forms on which the heroes of our Bible story looked in life. The reason of such a thing is that the Egyptians believed that when a man died, his soul, which passed to the life beyond, loved to return to its old home on earth, and find again the body in which it once dwelt; and even, perhaps, that the soul's existence in the other world depended in some way on the preservation of the body. So they made the bodies of their dead friends into what we call "mummies," steeping them for many days in pitch and spices till they were embalmed, and then wrapping them round in fold upon fold of fine linen. So they have endured all these hundreds of years, to be stored at last in a museum, and gazed upon by people who live in lands which were savage wildernesses when Egypt was a great and mighty Empire.

CHAPTER XIII

AN EGYPTIAN'S HEAVEN

In this chapter I want to tell you a little about what
the Egyptians thought of heaven--what it was,
where it was, how people got there after death, and
what kind of a life they lived when they were there.
They had some very quaint and curious ideas about
the heavens themselves. They believed, for
instance, that the blue sky overhead was something
like a great iron plate spread over the world, and
supported at the four corners, north, south, east, and
west, by high mountains. The stars were like little
lamps, which hung down from this plate. Right
round the world ran a great celestial river, and on
this river the sun sailed day after day in his bark,
giving light to the world. You could only see him as
he passed round from the east by the south to the
west, for after that the river ran behind high
mountains, and the sun passed out of sight to sail
through the world of darkness.

Behind the sun, and appearing after he had
vanished, came the moon, sailing in its own bark. It
was protected by two guardian eyes, which watched
always over it, and it needed the protection, for
every month it was attacked by a great enemy in the
form of a sow. For a fortnight the moon sailed on
safely, and grew fuller and rounder; but at the
middle of the month, just when it was full, the sow
attacked it, tore it out of its place, and flung it into
the celestial river, where for another fortnight it was
gradually extinguished, to be revived again at the
beginning of the next month. That was the

Egyptians' curious way of accounting for the
waxing and waning of the moon, and many of their
other ideas were just as quaint as this.

I do not mean to say anything of what they believed
about God, for they had so many gods, and believed
such strange things about them, that it would only
confuse you if I tried to make you understand it all.
But the most important thing in all the Egyptian
religion was the belief in heaven, and in the life
which people lived there after their life on earth was
ended. No other nation of these old times ever
believed so firmly as did the Egyptians that men
were immortal, and did not cease to be when they
died, but only began a new life, which might be
either happy or miserable, according to the way in
which they had lived on earth.

They had a lot of different beliefs about the life
after death, some of them rather confusing, and
difficult to understand; but I shall tell you only the
main things and the simplest things which they
believed. They said, then, that very long ago, when
the world was young, there was a great and good
King called Osiris, who reigned over Egypt, and
was very good to his subjects, teaching them all
kinds of useful knowledge. But Osiris had a wicked
brother named Set, who hated him, and was jealous
of him. One day Set invited Osiris to a supper, at
which he had gathered a number of his friends who
were in the plot with him. When they were all
feasting gaily, he produced a beautiful chest, and
offered to give it to the man who fitted it. One after
another they lay down in the chest, but it fitted none
of them. Then at last Osiris lay down in it, and as

soon as he was inside, his wicked brother and the other plotters fastened the lid down upon him, and threw the chest into the Nile. It was carried away by the river, and at last was washed ashore, with the dead body of the good King still in it.

But Isis, wife of Osiris, sought for her husband everywhere, and at last she found the chest with his body. While she was weeping over it the wicked Set came upon her, tore his brother's body to pieces, and scattered the fragments far and wide; but the faithful Isis traced them all, and buried them wherever she found them.

Now, Isis had a son named Horus, and when he grew to manhood he challenged Set, fought with him, and defeated him. Then the gods all assembled, and gave judgment that Osiris was in the right, and Set in the wrong. They raised Osiris up from the dead, made him a god, and appointed him to be judge of all men after death. And then, not all at once, but gradually, the Egyptians came to believe that because Osiris died, and rose again from the dead, and lived for ever after death, therefore all those men who believed in Osiris would live again after death, and dwell for ever with Osiris. You see that in some respects the story is strangely like that of the death and resurrection of Jesus Christ.

Well, then, they supposed that, when a man died on earth, after his body was mummified and laid in its tomb, his soul went on to the gates of the palace of Osiris in the other world, where was the Hall of Truth, in which souls were judged. The soul had to

know the magic names of the gates before it could
even enter the Hall; but as soon as these names
were spoken the gates opened, and the soul went in.
Within the Hall there stood a great pair of scales,
and beside the scales stood a god, ready to mark
down the result of the judgment; while all round the
Hall sat forty-two terrible creatures, who had
authority to punish particular sins.

The soul had to make confession to these avengers
of sin that he had not been guilty of the sins which
they had power to punish; then, when he had made
his confession, his heart was taken, and weighed in
the scales against a feather, which was the Egyptian
sign for truth. If it was not of the right weight, the
man was false, and his heart was thrown to a
dreadful monster, part crocodile, part
hippopotamus, which sat behind the balances, and
devoured the hearts of the unjust; but if it was right,
then Horus, the son of Osiris, took the man by the
hand, and led him into the presence of Osiris the
Judge, and he was pronounced just, and admitted to
heaven.

But what was heaven? Well, the Egyptians had
several different ideas about it. One rather pretty
one was that the souls which were pronounced just
were taken up into the sky, and there became stars,
shining down for ever upon the world. Another was
that they were permitted to enter the boat, in which,
as I told you, the sun sails round the world day by
day, and to keep company with the sun on his
unending voyage.

But the idea that most believed in and loved was

that somewhere away in a mysterious land to the west, there lay a wonderful and beautiful country, called the Field of Bulrushes. There the corn grew three and a half yards high, and the ears of corn were a yard long. Through the fields ran lovely canals, full of fish, and bordered with reeds and bulrushes. When the soul had passed the Judgment Hall, it came, by strange, hard roads, and through great dangers, to this beautiful country. And there the dead man, dead now no more, but living for ever, spent his time in endless peace and happiness, sowing and reaping, paddling in his canoe along the canals, or resting and playing draughts in the evening under the sycamore-trees.

Now, I suppose that all this seemed quite a happy sort of heaven to most of the common people, who had been accustomed all their days to hard work and harder fare; but by-and-by the great nobles came to think that a heaven of this sort was not quite good enough for them. They had never done any work on earth; why should they have to do any in heaven? So they thought that they would find out a way of taking their slaves with them into the other world. I fancy that at first they actually tried to take them by killing the slaves at their master's grave. When the funeral of a great man took place, some of his servants would be killed beside the tomb, so that they might go with their lord into heaven, and work for him there, as they had worked for him on earth.

But the Egyptians were always a gentle, kind-hearted people, and they quickly grew disgusted with the idea of such cruelty, so they found another way out of the difficulty. They got numbers of little clay figures made in the form of servants--one with a hoe on his shoulder, another with a basket in his hand, and so on. They called these little figures "Answerers," and when a man was buried, they buried a lot of these clay servants along with him, so that, when he reached heaven, and was summoned to do work in the Field of Bulrushes, the Answerers would rise up and answer for him, and take the task off his shoulders.

So, along with the mummies of the dead Egyptians, there is often found quite a number of these tiny figures, all ready to make heaven easy for their master when he gets there. They have sometimes a little verse written upon them, to tell the Answerer what he has got to do in the other world. It runs like this:

"Oh, thou Answerer, when I am called, and when I am asked to do any kind of work that is done in heaven, and am required at any time to cause the field to flourish, or to convey the sand from east to west, thou shalt say, 'Here am I.'"

It all seems rather a curious idea of heaven, does it not? And most curious of all is the idea of dodging work in the other world by carrying a bundle of china dolls to heaven with you. But, even if we think that very ridiculous, we need not forget that the Egyptians had a wonderfully clear and sure grasp of the fact that it is a man's character in this world which will make him either happy or unhappy in the next, and that evil-doing, even if it escapes punishment in this life, is a thing that God will surely punish at last.

Remember that these men of old, wonderfully wise and strong as they were in many ways, were still the children of the time when the world was young; like children, forming many false and even ridiculous ideas about things they could not understand; like children, too, reaching out their groping hands through the darkness to a Father whose love they felt, though they could not explain His ways. We need not wonder if at times they made mistakes, and went far astray. We may wonder far more at the way in which He taught them so many true and noble things and thoughts, never leaving Himself without a witness even in those days of long ago.

Made in the USA
Coppell, TX
05 May 2024